Puritanism: A Very Short Introduction

Very Short Introductions available now:

Available soon:

For more information visit our web site
www.oup.co.uk/general/vsi

Francis J. Bremer

PURITANISM

A Very Short Introduction

OXFORD
UNIVERSITY PRESS

Oxford University Press, Inc., publishes works that further
Oxford University's objective of excellence
in research, scholarship, and education.

Oxford New York

Auckland Cape Town Dar es Salaam Hong Kong Karachi
Kuala Lumpur Madrid Melbourne Mexico City Nairobi
New Delhi Shanghai Taipei Toronto

With offices in
Argentina Austria Brazil Chile Czech Republic France Greece
Guatemala Hungary Italy Japan Poland Portugal Singapore
South Korea Switzerland Thailand Turkey Ukraine Vietnam

Library of Congress Cataloging-in-Publication Data
Bremer, Francis J.
Puritanism : a very short introduction / Francis J. Bremer.
p. cm.—(Very short introductions)
Includes bibliographical references and index.
ISBN 978-0-19-533455-5 (pbk.)
1. Puritans. I. Title.
BX9323.B73 2009
285′.9—dc22
2008051697

Printed by Integrated Books International, United States of America
on acid-free paper

for my daughter Megan

Acknowledgments

Over the years my understanding of puritanism has been shaped not only by the many scholars who have written insightfully on the subject but also through numerous conversations. Christopher Hill was one of the first to encourage my interest in linking New England with the broader puritan world. John Morrill, Diarmaid MacCulloch, and Patrick Collinson have become good friends, while being generous in responding to my queries. Others in England who have helped me to understand the broader dimensions of puritanism include Tom Webster, John Coffey, Tom Freeman, John Craig, Ann Hughes, Jacqueline Eales, Jeremy Bangs, Alan Ford, and Malcolm Gaskill.

In the community of American puritan scholars I have been fortunate in the friendship and support of Michael McGiffert, Michael Winship, Stephen Foster, Alden Vaughan, David Hall, Charles Hambrick Stowe, Jeff Cooper, and Walt Woodward.

I am particularly grateful to John Spurr, who read an earlier version of this book and offered important advice. John Coffey and Paul Lim read a later draft to check for errors. My former student and current colleague Monica Spiese also provided useful feedback. Jane Mills, John Goldsmith, and Richard Trask were helpful in identifying the images used. And I would like to thank

Susan Ferber and Nancy Toff at Oxford University Press for their help in making this a better book than it otherwise would have been. This is the second book I have published with that press, and I have been fortunate in both cases to have had Joellyn Ausanka as production editor. I wish to thank her for her careful and perceptive work on the manuscript.

For thirty-one years I have been attempting to explain the puritans to my students at Millersville University of Pennsylvania. Their interest and responses have assisted me in finding ways to make the world of John Winthrop and his fellow saints intelligible to the men and women of today. And finally, I wish to thank them and also my fellow scholar-teachers in the Millersville History Department.

Contents

List of illustrations

Introduction

The relationship between religious faith and political culture has long been a staple of public discourse. "Puritans" and "puritanism" are terms likely to be invoked in such discussions, despite being references to centuries-old religious subjects. Nevertheless, puritanism is one of the least understood parts of America's—and Britain's—heritage. The word "puritan" is likely to be associated with "prudish," "sexually repressed," "prohibitionist," "busybody snoops"—the types of things that led the twentieth-century social critic H. L. Mencken to define puritanism as "the fear that someone, somewhere, may be happy." The image of puritans as theocrats, regicides, witch-burners, Indian killers, and bigoted heresy hunters has long been entrenched in popular culture. Most of these are distortions if not absolute falsehoods, but the stereotypes are deeply embedded.

The purpose of this *Very Short Introduction* is to present the puritans as they were, to provide a clear explanation of what they believed, how they worshipped, how they lived their everyday lives and interacted with their fellow believers and the broader world, and why the movement as such came to an end. But more fundamentally, it will help us to consider again some of the issues that the men and women of the seventeenth century took seriously—the proper relationship between religion and public life, the limits of toleration, and the balance between individual rights and community obligations. It seeks to explain both the common elements of the movement and the distinct character it assumed in different times and places.

Among the most fundamental yet disputed aspects of the subject is the definition of puritanism. Whereas other religious movements of the sixteenth and seventeenth centuries—Lutheranism, Catholicism, Genevan Calvinism, among others—became institutionalized so that there were official statements of faith and formal membership in churches, puritanism never achieved that type of clear identity. It was a movement defined in part by the self-identification of men and women who referred to themselves as "godly" or "professors" and partly by their enemies, who scorned them as "precisians," and "hypocrites." The actual label "puritan" was originally a term of opprobrium used by their enemies, though eventually adopted by the members of the movement. Some scholars have come to look at puritanism as a temperament and to talk of the "puritan character." Recent research points to the varieties of puritanism, pointing out that the experience, beliefs, and behavior of these believers was often uniquely shaped by particular circumstances they faced.

At the simplest level, puritans were those who sought to reform themselves and their society by purifying their churches of the remnants of Roman Catholic teachings and practice then found in post-Reformation England during the mid-sixteenth century, such as using clerical vestments and kneeling to receive the Lord's Supper. They were particularly insistent that individual believers had access to the Scriptures, the Word of God, in their own language. They agitated for the placement of university-trained preachers in every parish. They believed that England as a political nation must be committed to opposing the forces of Rome throughout Christendom. While Englishmen who were not labeled puritans might support some or all of these objectives, those who bore the label were seen as most committed and most fervent in advancing them.

At the heart of puritanism was the attempt to transform society by first using grace to make God's will one's own. By doing so the individual would lead an exemplary life that would persuade others—family, friends, and the broader community—to follow the path of right belief and behavior. When puritans achieved political power—in America in the colonies they established and in England following the Civil Wars of the 1640s—they were able to employ instruments of power as well as those of persuasion. The responsibilities that came with power brought new challenges but did not alter the puritan objective to make society a godly kingdom. Their understanding of God's will led them to promote education, to redefine marriage and other institutions, and to adopt participatory forms of government. While puritans as a specific group are no longer with us, the impact of those initiatives on America and England continues to be felt.

Chapter 1
Reforming the English Reformation

Puritanism did not begin as a distinct faith but as a reform movement within the Protestant Church of England in the sixteenth century. Puritans were Christian men and women who sought to shape their lives in accordance with God's will. They believed they were required by God to spread their belief and practice to others by word and example—to turn their families, their communities, and their larger societies into parts of the kingdom of God. From the first stirrings of the movement until the 1630s, puritan efforts took place within the established national church and were shaped by broader struggles to define that church.

The Church of England was shaped by Henry VIII's break from the Roman Catholic Church in 1534. The Church of England differed from the other Protestant churches of the time in that the reasons for its formation were political rather than spiritual. Henry VIII rejected the authority of the Roman Catholic Church because Pope Clement VII refused to annul his marriage to Catherine of Aragon. Yet Henry was far from convinced of the need to change Catholic teachings or worship. He would have been well content to have a new church with the intellectual and ceremonial furnishings of the old. But the men willing to run his church believed in many of the new ideas of the Reformation regarding decentralized church authority, the importance of faith as opposed to works in the pathway to salvation, and rejection of many of the traditional sacraments. In Henry's reign a debate began over the nature of the new church that would continue for over a century.

Thomas Cromwell, Henry's principal lay advisor in matters concerning the church, persuaded the king to suppress many of the country's monasteries. In the process, considerable church lands and associated powers were transferred into lay hands, and many Englishmen obtained a financial stake in the new church. Cromwell also persuaded Henry to authorize an English Bible. Thomas Cranmer, holder of the Church of England's highest position as the archbishop of Canterbury, was an advocate of religious reform. He led those, referred to as evangelicals, who sought to persuade the king to accept the Protestant concept of justification by faith (as opposed to good works), to reject the Catholic doctrine of transubstantiation (the belief that Christ is substantively present in the bread and wine of Communion), and to revise the liturgy. His success was limited by the king's own conservative instincts and the lobbying of other Englishmen who wanted as little change as possible.

The accession of the boy-king Edward VI in 1547 was a godsend for those seeking further reform. Tutored by men who were zealous advocates of evangelical reform, Edward gave his approval to various steps long favored by such men. Shrines that honored saints were closed, religious statues that Protestants believed promoted idolatry were destroyed or defaced, church wall paintings whitewashed, stained glass windows depicting religious scenes replaced, and musical instruments sold off, vandalized, or destroyed. Cranmer's reformed vernacular liturgy, the Book of Common Prayer, was approved. The archbishop installed the noted continental reformers Martin Bucer and Peter Martyr in theological chairs at Cambridge and Oxford, respectively, where they helped to shape the views of a new generation of clergy. A second Prayer Book, issued in 1552, reflected further progress toward bringing England into line with the Reformation in Europe.

Even under Edward, however, the pace of reform was insufficient for many. John Hooper was typical of such men. He initially turned down an appointment as Bishop of Gloucester because he believed the oath he would be required to take and the vestments he would be expected to wear were papist remnants. After he relented and was installed, he continued to lobby Cranmer for more thorough reformation. In the eyes of many, such individuals who remained in the national church but demanded a faster, more thorough purification of the church were the earliest puritans.

The failure of Cranmer and the king to go further in reforming the Church of England owed much to the opposition of those Englishmen who still retained an allegiance for the faith and practices of the old religion, sentiments that contributed to popular uprisings during the reigns of both Henry VIII and Edward VI. The strength of such sentiment became obvious when Edward died in 1553 and was succeeded by his sister, Mary Tudor. Mary, the daughter of Henry VIII and Catherine of Aragon, was determined to restore England to the Roman Catholic Church. Nearly three hundred English men and women who refused to abandon their Protestant faith, including Cranmer and Hooper, were burned as heretics. Another eight hundred fled to centers of reform on the Continent, forming their own churches and engaging in dialogue with Protestant leaders in places such as Geneva, Zurich, Frankfurt, and Strasbourg. An undetermined number of Protestants stayed in England and sought to practice their reformed faith in underground gatherings.

Mary died in 1558 and was succeeded by her sister, Elizabeth, the last surviving child of Henry VIII, who restored Protestantism to the realm and, through her longevity, did much to assure its permanence. It was during the four decades of Elizabeth's reign that the puritan movement is generally regarded as achieving a significant place in English religious life. Recognizing the strength of conservative sentiment (much of it Catholic or pseudo-Catholic),

Elizabeth insisted on a religious settlement that was slightly more moderate than the state of the church at the death of Edward VI. This was a disappointment to those who had returned from exile eager to reproduce some of the practices they had observed on the Continent. Some of these men reluctantly accepted positions of authority in the Elizabethan church in the hope that they could use their power and influence to advocate further reform. Others, unwilling to accept the responsibility to enforce what they viewed as unscriptural practices, took lesser posts in the church as parish rectors or lecturers, where they might escape the attention of the authorities and institute reform on the local level.

The reform agenda during Elizabeth's reign focused on four major matters: doctrine, ceremonial practices, a preaching ministry, and opposition to Roman Catholic power. Underlying their position on these issues were two general emphases. The first was a belief in the inerrancy of the Scriptures, which led puritans more than most Protestants to seek scriptural warrant for all of their beliefs and practices. The second was anti-Catholicism. For the puritans, more than many of their fellow English Protestants, the papacy was the source of all doctrinal and ceremonial errors that had taken the church off the course initially set by Christ and his early disciples.

Calvinism—the system of beliefs that were developed by the Protestant John Calvin in Geneva—became the doctrinal preference of most English Protestants, and reformers were largely pleased with the incorporation of this viewpoint in the official pronouncements of the Elizabethan bishops and the curriculum of the English universities. Not until later in Elizabeth's reign were these teachings openly challenged in the universities, and even then the authorities remained committed to Calvinist doctrines.

The most notable division between what the church required and what the puritans desired came over the issue of ceremonies. Puritans wished to dispense with the elaborate clerical vestments that symbolized a priesthood of special powers. They wished clergy to officiate in simple black gowns, a badge of their university training. Because they believed that kneeling at Communion symbolized a recognition of the real presence of Christ in the bread and wine being distributed (which they denied), they preferred to sit or stand to receive the Lord's Supper. They wished to dispense with the signing of the cross over infants in baptism and the exchange of rings in matrimony, seeing both as Catholic symbols. Parishes with a strong puritan element were more likely to remove rood screens and rename the altar a Communion table, moving it from the chancel to the nave of the church for congregants to gather around. They preferred their minister to pray extemporaneously rather than use the set forms of the Book of Common Prayer. In regions of England where authorities were sympathetic or indifferent to such issues, puritans could often initiate such reforms with little fear of being corrected. One did not have to be a puritan to favor such changes.

Significant steps were taken in Elizabeth's reign to prepare an educated ministry. Emmanuel College at Cambridge was founded specifically to meet the demand for preaching clergy, but other colleges at Oxford and Cambridge also produced puritan clergy. When a local minister was unable to provide the spiritual nourishment puritans demanded, parishioners might engage in what was called sermon gadding, traveling to a nearby village to hear an effective preacher. Some communities funded lectureships, hiring a noted preacher to offer public sermons for those whose appetite for the Word seemed insatiable. Early in Elizabeth's reign many bishops organized or approved exercises called prophesyings. This was a means of upgrading the knowledge and skills of those ministers who had not received university training. Clergy in the region would gather to be instructed by a learned minister. Occasionally, laypeople were included in the sessions. While never denying the ideal of an educated ministry, Elizabeth had reservations about clergy who chose what to preach about and what to say, preferring that they read the homilies set forth in the officially provided Book of Homilies. Seeing prophesying as

8

potentially subversive, she ordered Archbishop of Canterbury Edmund Grindal to suppress the exercises and suspended him from his functions when he refused. Godly ministers responded to the suppression of prophesyings by organizing their own informal conferences to discuss and achieve consensus on how to interpret the Scriptures, how to respond to government indifference to further reform, and how to best regulate the affairs of their parishes.

Few puritans could fault Elizabeth on her opposition to Rome. She became known as "the Protestant Deborah" (after the Old Testament heroine) for her aggressively Protestant foreign policy. She supported the Protestant rebels in the Netherlands and encouraged English privateers to prey upon Catholic Spain's treasure fleets and its American colonies. The simmering hostility between the two countries eventually led to Spain's attempt to invade and subjugate England in 1588. When Elizabeth's ships fought off the Armada, Englishmen saw their triumph as a sign of God's favor.

Puritans were not necessarily opposed to government of the church by bishops and initially showed a willingness to cooperate with those bishops who were sympathetic to reform. But as time went on most bishops proved either unwilling to challenge the queen or eager to carry out her demands on such matters as the wearing of vestments. Puritan clergy began to organize their own informal associations or conferences to advance their positions and provide authorization for their views, such as the one formed in Dedham, in the Stour Valley borderland of Essex and Suffolk. Some members of these conferences suggested that the church be remodeled along Presbyterian lines such as were to be found in Scotland. Two London clergymen, John Field and Thomas Wilcox, led a campaign to persuade Parliament to institute such reforms, but Elizabeth denied Parliament's right to change the church. Field also played a key role in trying to connect the various puritan clerical conferences through an informal national system. Walter

Travers prepared a *Book of Discipline*, which set forth a model for the type of reforms these men advocated. While generally referred to as a Presbyterian movement, the various conferences were all unofficial and thus were only advisory rather than having authority over their members.

By the time Elizabeth died, puritans had failed to persuade the nation's political and ecclesiastical governors to adopt the reforms they advocated, although they had attracted an increasing number of English men and women, spreading their message beyond themselves and their families. In some areas, such as the Stour Valley, the support of local authorities had allowed the creation of what some extolled as a "kingdom of God" in which puritanism was the hegemonic religious culture. In other areas, puritan strongholds were more tenuous, leading to sharper distinctions between the godly, gathered in what the historian Patrick Collinson has called "holy huddles," and their more worldly neighbors.

In 1603 the English throne passed to Elizabeth's kinsman, James Stuart, who had been king of Scotland. Scotland's church was Presbyterian, and puritans hoped that this would make the new monarch sympathetic to their proposed reforms. They gathered as many as a thousand signatures on a petition to the king, who responded by calling the Hampton Court Conference to consider the state of the English church. James had clashed with the Scottish church, which was independent of the crown, and he was attracted to the English system, which placed the monarch in charge. He rejected most of the puritan requests, though he did make provision for a new translation of the Bible—which became known as the Authorized Version, or the King James Bible. During the reign of Queen Elizabeth the distinction between the establishment and puritan reformers was not always clear since many bishops and key members of the Queen's Privy Council were sympathetic to further reforms in the church. Under James I and

A Puritan in England

In the village where I lived the reader read the Common Prayer briefly, and the rest of the day even till dark night almost, except eating-time, was spent in dancing under a maypole and a great tree not far from my father's door, where all the town did meet together.... We could not read the Scripture in our family without the great disturbance of the tabor and pipe and noise in the street. Many times my mind was inclined to be among them, and sometimes I broke loose from conscience and joined with them; and the more I did it the more I was inclined to it. But when I heard them call my father Puritan it did much to cure me and alienate me from them; for I considered that my father's exercise of reading the Scripture was better than theirs, and would surely be better thought on by all men at the last; and I considered what it was for that he and others were thus derided.

Source: N. H. Keeble, ed., *The Autobiography of Richard Baxter* (London: Dent, 1974).

his son and heir Charles I, friends of the puritans were less likely to be found at court or in bishops' palaces.

James, however, was more intent on asserting his right to make decisions than he was energetic in making sure those decisions were implemented. Archbishop Richard Bancroft did make efforts to force puritans to conform to the rites and ceremonies stipulated in the Prayer Book, and some puritan clergy were suspended for refusing to wear vestments or similar acts of nonconformity. But puritan clergy were often the most capable and zealous in a diocese, and this led many bishops to reach accommodations with them. Throughout the country privately funded church lectureships provided new opportunities for puritan preachers to nourish the faith of the godly and to reach out to those who still embraced error. Puritans continued to find little to complain about regarding the Calvinist foundations of the church. James was himself a Calvinist and appointed the Calvinist George Abbot to replace Bancroft as archbishop of Canterbury. When the Calvinist authorities in the Netherlands convened an international synod at Dort in 1618 to examine the controversial teachings of Jacob Arminius (who argued that man did have a role in his own salvation), James sent a delegation that joined the majority in rejecting the views of Arminius and reaffirmed the key elements of Calvinism.

As long as they felt confident in the Calvinist foundations of the Church, most puritan clergy were willing to mute their public criticisms of ceremonies they disapproved of in order to maintain a common front against the Catholic threats to the Reformation. Pastors and lecturers devoted themselves to "practical divinity," preaching and writing guidance to individual Christians to help them live godly lives. They hoped to reform their neighborhoods and the broader society by their example and their teachings. Works of practical divinity became emblematic of English puritanism and influenced Continental reformers in the Netherlands and as far away as Hungary.

Not all of the godly were willing to make compromises while waiting for the king to approve needed reforms. Some began to separate from the national church and hold their own meetings for worship. Because all Englishmen were required by law to attend parish services, by absenting themselves (as many Catholics also did), the Separatists left themselves open to prosecution. Some, such as Henry Barrow and John Greenwood, were executed. Separatists were critical of the puritans who refused to follow their way; puritans, responding to charges that separatism was the natural outcome of their own positions, attacked the Separatists in pulpit and print. Over time many Separatist groups migrated to the Netherlands, seeking there the freedom to worship as they pleased. One of these groups originated in the region of Scrooby, settled in Leiden, and then migrated to America in 1620, where they became known as the Pilgrims.

Puritans of all kinds were committed to the cause of international Protestantism and had concerns about King James's foreign policy. He had brought an end to England's war with Spain and showed a willingness to deal with the great Catholic powers. When the Thirty Years War broke out on the Continent in 1618, James refused to provide military aid to his son-in law Frederick, the proclaimed king of Bohemia, even though Frederick was the Protestant champion in a conflict many thought was the climactic struggle to determine the religious future of Europe. Puritans increasingly criticized the government's stand and, on their own initiative, raised funds to help Protestants dislocated by the conflict.

At the same time that the spirit of Separatism challenged traditional puritanism, a new cadre of churchmen came to prominence who sought their own changes in the national Church. Lancelot Andrewes, Richard Neile, and William Laud began to promote "the beauty of holiness," a program that included ceremonies such as kneeling to receive the Lord's Supper, the return of altars to the chancel, Communion rails, fine music in worship, and other elements that evoked memories of discarded Catholic practices. Some of these men, and their allies such as George Montagu and John Cosin, also sought to challenge the accepted teachings on predestination. Puritan concerns about an anti-Calvinist conspiracy to move England back toward Rome were accentuated when King James married his son and heir Charles to a French Catholic princess and bestowed on her the right to have open Catholic worship at the court. The more puritans questioned royal policy, the more James came to appreciate and promote men such as Neile, who were staunch advocates of royal authority. Puritan clergy such as John Preston, who had been favored by the king early in his reign, began to lose influence. This trend intensified after the accession of Charles I in 1625. The resultant challenges would force puritans to develop new strategies if they were to survive and advance God's kingdom.

Chapter 2
Puritan experiments

As king, Charles I took unprecedented steps to roll back puritan influence, forcing many individuals and communities to reconsider how to reconcile their commitment to God's cause and their membership in the national church. Eventually these policies would lead many puritans to migrate to New England in the 1630s, where they would seek to advance God's kingdom in a number of new colonies. The growing divisions between puritans and the king would contribute to the outbreak of the English Civil Wars (1642–51) that ultimately led to a rule of the puritan saints (as they called themselves) in the 1640s and 1650s. In New England and England, puritans for the first time would be presented with the opportunity to advance their views by mandate as opposed to persuasion. These two experiments in shaping godly rule would bring new challenges that would alter the nature of puritanism.

During the first decade of Charles's reign the rift between the puritans and the church hierarchy grew. Traditional Calvinist teachings were undermined. Controversial innovations in worship that many believed harkened back to Catholic practice were introduced. Altars were required to be railed in and communicants instructed to kneel to receive the Sacrament. Churchgoers were expected to stand during the Creed, the Epistle, and the Gospel. Wearing hats in church, a common practice, was forbidden.

Bishops were less tolerant of nonconformity and more energetic in enforcing the use of disputed ceremonies. Sports and other recreations, which the puritans had sought to ban on the Sabbath, were explicitly allowed by royal authority. Lectureships, which gave puritan clergy a pulpit to preach their views without requiring them to participate in disputed ceremonies, were subject to new controls. Some lectureships were closed down by the authorities. Puritans in parish ministries found that conformity was no longer negotiable with local bishops. Some ministers were suspended, others were deprived of their livings, and still others recognized an impending threat.

The ways in which men and women understood these challenges was influenced by their view of the key issues of their times. All Christians believed that all history moved toward the climactic struggle between the forces of Christ and Antichrist foretold in the book of Revelation and the dawn of the millennial rule of the saints. Many Englishmen viewed the events of the Reformation in general and the Thirty Years War in particular as important parts of this struggle. Those puritans who had muted their public criticisms of the English Church had done so in order to maintain a common front against the Catholic threat. Archbishop William Laud was instrumental in establishing in the Church of England certain practices that resembled Roman Catholic worship, further alienating puritans. They perceived Laudian innovations in proper belief and practice undermining England's solidarity with the Protestant cause, and this perspective made conformity even more difficult.

Many puritans began to consider emigration. This had always been a means by which religious dissenters could escape the control of the church authorities and bide their time abroad as they waited for a possible change in the religious climate. English Protestants fleeing persecution during the reign of Queen Mary and reformers threatened by the authorities in Elizabeth's reign had journeyed to the Continent and eventually returned. In the early seventeenth century the Netherlands was the most attractive refuge for English puritans. Regiments of English volunteers were commanded by officers such as Sir Horace Vere who were sympathetic to religious reform and employed puritans as chaplains. Communities of English and Scots merchants existed in all the major Dutch cities and towns, including the company of Merchant Adventurers in Antwerp and Middleburg, and the Dutch authorities allowed these groups to organize their own churches. There were over two dozen such English congregations in the Netherlands by 1630. For the most part these churches conducted their own affairs and selected their own clergy.

As many Englishmen would migrate to the Netherlands in the years before 1640 as would go to the Americas in the 1630s. Yet in the years when puritans in England were subject to growing pressures to conform, various factors made the Netherlands less attractive as a refuge. The end of the Dutch truce with Spain coincided with the outbreak of the Thirty Years War, making emigration to the Netherlands potentially dangerous, especially for those with families. At the same time, the English government applied growing pressure on the Dutch authorities to crack down on the autonomy of puritan congregations.

Ireland offered another option for emigration. Created by Henry VIII at the time when he broke from Rome, the Protestant Church of Ireland was distinct from the English Church. Long delays in translating the Bible and the liturgy into the native Gaelic tongue, and the inability of the new protestant clergy to preach in that language, doomed the effort to convert the local population to the Protestant faith. But the church did minister to the new English immigrants who were settling not only around Dublin but also in the plantations established in the late sixteenth and early seventeenth centuries in the southwest (Munster) and northeast (Ulster) regions of the island. Led by bishops such as James Ussher, the Irish Church had won a reputation as being more in keeping with the type of church puritans sought. The Suffolk gentleman John Winthrop invested in an Irish plantation, sent his son to study at Trinity College, Dublin, and considered emigration there himself. Yet even as Winthrop and other English puritans pondered leaving England, the attractiveness of that haven began to diminish. King James decided to assert his authority over the Irish Church, and then Charles I approved a number of concessions to Irish Catholics that cast doubt on the future of Protestantism there as in England.

The Earl of Warwick and other puritans had been involved in overseas colonizing ventures such as the Virginia Company, but their early efforts were driven by economic rather than religious concerns. That soon began to change. In 1614 the puritan leaders of the Bermuda Company sent Lewis Hughes to that island, where he instituted forms of worship that ignored the Book of Common Prayer. Some of the same men would be involved in the Providence Island Company, which attempted to establish a puritan colony in the western Caribbean in the 1630s. The Pilgrims, of course, were seeking a religious refuge when they settled Plymouth in 1620. By the end of that decade, puritans in the southwest of England who had established a New England outpost as a profit-making fishing enterprise began to think of the possibility of a religious refuge in the New World. Joining with others, they reorganized their enterprise as the Massachusetts Bay Company, receiving a royal charter in 1629.

For all of those who considered emigration in light of the new attacks on puritanism, the decision to leave England was not an easy one. It meant cutting themselves off from many family and friends and adjusting to new patterns of life in an unfamiliar land. Some of their fellow believers were quick to condemn clergy who emigrated as deserters who were willing to abandon their flocks and give up the fight for reform. Many ministers saw no option, however. They had been willing to make compromises to stay and nourish their flocks in earlier years but now found it increasingly

1. John Endecott (d. 1655) was one of the leading magistrates of the new colony of Massachusetts and occasionally governor of the colony.

difficult to continue. Staying would mean accepting unpopular innovations in religious practice, and those who had counted on the tolerance of local bishops could no longer do so. In London and in England's counties, many clergy and laymen concluded that they had no choice but to leave.

In 1630 John Winthrop led the first ships of the Great Migration to New England. In his lay sermon to those who were embarking on this expedition with him, "A Model of Christian Charity," Winthrop sought to unite those who came from different parts of England and different puritan experiences to form a single community. He told them that they had entered into a covenant with each other and with God. They were required to sacrifice their individual aspirations for the common good, to live exemplary Christian lives, caring for one another and struggling alongside each other to create due forms of civil and spiritual life. If they maintained this commitment to God and to one another, God would reward them with peace and prosperity. Just as godly individuals living exemplary lives stirred others to follow them, so New England would be as a "City Upon a Hill," which others would seek to emulate. If they failed to uphold their bargain with God, the Lord would punish them.

The colonists who followed Winthrop were faced with the dangers of a difficult ocean voyage and the challenges of creating communities in the wilderness—building their own homes,

John Winthrop on "Christian Charity"

We are a Company professing ourselves fellow members of Christ, in which respect only, though we were absent from each other many miles, and had our employments as far distant, yet we ought to account our selves knit together by this bond of love, and live in the exercise of it. . . . In such cases as this the care of the public must oversway all private respects. . . . We must be knit together in this work as one man. We must entertain each other in brotherly Affection. We must be willing to abridge ourselves of our superfluities, for the supply of others necessities. We must uphold a familiar Commerce together in all meekness, gentleness, patience, and liberality. We must delight in each other, make others Conditions our own, rejoice together, mourn together, labor and suffer together, always having before our eyes our Commission and Community in the work, our Community as members of the same body.

Source: Samuel Eliot Morison, ed., *Winthrop Papers, Volume II: 1623–1630* (Boston: Massachusetts Historical Society, 1931).

adapting to a strange environment, starting from scratch in raising their own food. But they were also challenged to create a godly kingdom. Over the first decade they developed a colonial government in which freemen (soon limited to church members) annually elected their governor as well as representatives to an upper legislative house and deputies to sit in a lower house. Town meetings of local householders managed the affairs of their individual communities and chose local officeholders. Churches were organized according to congregational principles, with each community selecting its religious leaders and organizing a local congregation of those believed to be God's elect. That congregation then admitted new members and determined its own affairs. Clerical conferences, comparable to those that had brought English puritan clergy together to discuss common issues, were instituted in New England to help the separate congregations strive toward unity. Some English puritans believed that the colonial churches were drifting toward separatism, but the colonists continually asserted their membership in the national church.

Unity was the goal of the New England puritans, but not necessarily uniformity. Winthrop had expressed the hope that if the colonists adhered to their covenant, God would grant them a better understanding of his ways and his wishes. Dialogue to facilitate a better apprehension of the truth was generally welcomed in early Massachusetts, though this search was on occasion put at risk by the intolerance of those who believed they had already found the truth and that no other views could be tolerated. Such intransigence could come from both sides of the religious spectrum. Roger Williams was as intolerant as those who had banished him from Massachusetts in 1634 when he insisted that the colony had no right to require oaths of freemen and no authority to legislate Sabbath behavior, that the churches must renounce any connection with the English Church, and that clerical conferences threatened the autonomy of individual congregations. He moved south and founded the town of Providence, in what would become Rhode Island.

In 1636 Thomas Shepard, the pastor of the Newtown (later Cambridge) church, became convinced that the religious discussions going on in the Boston church were too dangerous to be tolerated. His attack on Anne Hutchinson, Henry Vane, and other members of the Boston congregation who espoused a direct spiritual connection with God ended up polarizing the colony. Hutchinson's supporters became convinced that the majority of the colony's clergy were overemphasizing the role of works in the process of salvation and thus spiritually starving the colonists. Among the views they espoused were notions of free grace that struck many as being a form of the dangerous heresy of Antinomianism, which denied any correlation between the worth of the individual and obedience to laws. A synod of New England churches did not set forth a list of what people were required to believe, but rather a list of unacceptable doctrines. Moderates such as Winthrop tried to hold the center, but the antagonism between the extremists on both sides threatened the civil as well as the religious peace of Massachusetts. Anne Hutchinson was not merely seeking freedom to believe as she wished; she was publicly maintaining that the views of the majority of the clergy were false, harmful to the spiritual welfare of the colonists, and should be prohibited. In such a contest only one side could prevail, and Hutchinson was banished from the colony and excommunicated from the Boston church. A number of men and women followed her to establish settlements in Rhode Island. Most of those who had been in sympathy with her, including the Boston clergyman John Cotton, to whom she had pointed as her inspiration, were drawn back within the perimeter fence of orthodoxy.

Rhode Island was not the only offshoot of Massachusetts. The clergyman Thomas Hooker led townsmen from Newtown to settle along the Connecticut River. Along with some colonists sent by English peers who had considered establishing their own puritan refuge, they formed the colony of Connecticut. The London puritan John Davenport, who had spent some time in the Netherlands, led a group of English puritans who founded the New Haven colony (which would be merged into Connecticut in 1662). During the first few decades of its history, Massachusetts gradually extended its control over settlements along the northeastern New England frontier, in what would later become New Hampshire and Maine.

During their years of growth, the puritan colonies also faced serious external problems. Conflicting territorial claims by different English colonists, the Dutch New Netherlands colony, and separate tribes of Native Americans created a very volatile situation along the Connecticut River, which led to the Pequot War in 1636. The English colonists and their native allies destroyed the Pequot tribe, in the process introducing Native Americans to the savagery of European warfare of this period, setting fire to the principal Pequot fort, and killing women and children along with warriors. The future of these "Bible Commonwealths" (the colonies of Massachusetts, Plymouth, Connecticut, and New Haven) was also threatened by growing attention from the English government. Following his elevation to archbishop of Canterbury, William Laud began to devote attention to colonial affairs and took steps to curtail emigration to the colonies and to seek recall of the Massachusetts charter. The colonists prepared to defend themselves against the possible imposition of a royal governor, but were spared by the outbreak of conflict in the three British kingdoms.

During the period of New England's settlement, puritans who remained in England grew increasingly disaffected. Their responses to the worsening situation they found themselves in would contribute to civil wars in the 1640s. Charles I had not only sought to bring the English congregations in the Netherlands and the Irish church into closer alignment with the practices of the Church of England, but he had tried as well to reshape the Church of Scotland along English lines. His actions in Scotland prompted violent protests in 1638 and an outpouring of support for a National Covenant, which pledged those Scots who swore to it to withstand changes to their national church. Charles's initial effort to suppress the uprising failed. After having governed without a parliament for eleven years (the Personal Rule), the king was forced to call parliamentary elections in 1640.

During that Personal Rule the king had violated what many Englishmen believed were their rights, particularly in the ways he had raised revenues, but without a Parliament there had been no forum in which Englishmen could seek redress of grievances. When the parliament elected in 1640 (called the Short Parliament) refused to provide the funds the king needed to suppress the Scottish uprising without his agreeing to respond to the complaints of his subjects, Charles dissolved the body and sought to fight his northern subjects anyway. Again he was defeated, which forced him to call elections for what became known as the Long Parliament.

While offering hope to puritans, the initial focus of those who sat in the new parliament was pursuing the political grievances that had accumulated over the previous decade. Wielding the power of the purse, they forced the king to accept various constitutional reforms, including the Triennial Act, which required regular parliaments, and the abolition of various prerogative courts and prerogative taxation. One of the king's key advisors, the Earl of Strafford, was executed and other advisors and judges impeached or forced into exile. Parliament then accepted and debated a Root and Branch Petition, which demanded church reforms that puritans had agitated for, and their principal foe, Archbishop Laud, was imprisoned. These matters were pushed to the side for a time by an Irish rebellion and the widespread massacre of Protestant settlers there. This required the dispatch of military forces, but Parliament and the king could not agree on who should have control of the army. After failing to seize the ringleaders of the parliamentary opposition, in 1642 Charles raised his standard and called upon loyal Englishmen to assist him in opposing Parliament. The English Civil Wars had begun.

Because of the importance of religious issues in this struggle it has been referred to by some historians as "the Puritan Revolution," and by others as a War of Religion. Certainly it was puritans who were foremost in promoting the parliamentary cause. A year after hostilities began, Parliament entered into an alliance, the Solemn League and Covenant, with the Scots. After three years of indecisive conflict, Parliament reorganized its forces in 1645, and the New Model Army soon won a decisive victory, forcing the king to surrender in 1646.

While the early military campaigns were being conducted, in 1643 puritans had pushed through Parliament a call for a clerical gathering to debate the reformation of the English Church. The deliberations at that Westminster Assembly led to a broad affirmation of Calvinist principles (the Westminster Confession of Faith). The debates also revealed a growing fissure in the puritan movement. Never having had the power to change the church, puritans were divided as to what system of church government would best advance God's kingdom. Some advocated Presbyterian style reforms, while others supported Congregationalism, commonly referred to as the New England Way. One of the concerns the delegates faced was how well each of these systems might control the growing number of sects that had arisen in England in the absence of any central control over religious matters.

The brief history of the American puritan experiment was examined by Englishmen for what light it might shed on these issues. Advocates of Presbyterianism pointed to the emergence of heretics like Anne Hutchinson as evidence of the weakness of Congregationalism, while the English supporters of the New England Way emphasized the success of the colonists in controlling dissent. New England clerical authors such as John

Cotton, John Davenport, and Thomas Hooker became deeply engaged in these debates. When the Assembly recommended Presbyterianism to Parliament, the Congregationalists published *An Apologetical Narration* seeking the right to have their congregations remain independent of such a national church. Over the following years they formed an alliance of convenience with sects that also sought a measure of religious freedom, and this "Independent" coalition obstructed the implementation of a Presbyterian establishment ordered by Parliament in 1644. Although they were divided, all of these groups were heirs of and promoters of the puritan tradition.

Negotiations between Charles I and Parliament dragged on inconclusively following the king's surrender in 1645, during which time radical forces within the army, called the Levellers, began to agitate for a broader suffrage, regular parliaments, a transfer of power in the direction of the House of Commons, and the guarantee of various rights including freedom of religion. These issues were aired in discussions between representatives of the troops and the army leadership, including Oliver Cromwell, known as the Putney Debates of October 1647. These developments fueled Scottish disenchantment with Parliament's failure to effectively impose Presbyterianism, something they believed their English allies had promised. This gave Charles I an opportunity, and in 1648 he escaped confinement and reached an agreement with some of the Scottish leaders.

In the Second Civil War, the English Army made short work of the king and his new allies. Parliament was then purged and the remaining members (the Rump) voted to put the king on trial. Charles was convicted of crimes against his people and executed in January 1649. Parliament declared England a Commonwealth, but the ineffectiveness of Parliament over the following years led Oliver Cromwell to dissolve the Rump and institute the Protectorate of England in 1653. Cromwell had steadily risen as a figure of importance during the First Civil War, had been a key figure in defeating the king's forces in the Second Civil War, had suppressed the Irish revolt (through draconian measures), and defeated the Scots after they rebelled on behalf of Charles I's son and heir. A fervent puritan whom many saw as an instrument of God, Cromwell would dominate English affairs through the 1650s.

OLIVER Lord Protector of the Commonwealth of England, Scotland, and Ireland &
Sould by P. Stent

2. Oliver Cromwell (1599–1658) played a key role in the military triumph of Parliament in the English Civil Wars and governed the nation as Lord Protector for much of the 1650s.

Cromwell's Protectorate represented England's experiment in puritan rule. He provided England with a stable government and made the country one of the foremost European powers. He sent an expedition to attack Catholic Spain's New World empire, which, though thwarted in its broader ambitions, brought Jamaica into the British Empire. He developed a religious settlement, which relied upon the cooperation of Congregationalists, moderate Presbyterians, and some Baptists to provide a reformed parish ministry. Religious toleration was broad but not unlimited. Cromwell attempted to advance moral reform and a culture of discipline by appointing Major-Generals responsible for different parts of the land. Unable to find a fully workable system of national government that would be consistent in advancing God's kingdom, he nevertheless rejected offers of the crown, which might have brought stability to the land.

A man of extraordinary stature and charisma, Cromwell was able to control the royalist, republican, Leveller, and other forces in England's political life. His death in 1658 led to virtual anarchy. No other puritan was able to gain control of the nation, and in 1660 the eldest son of Charles I was invited back to England and crowned as Charles II (1660–85). The Parliament convened by the new monarch proved far more unforgiving than the king himself, rejecting any accommodation of puritans in the reestablished Church of England. Puritanism became "dissent" or "nonconformity" as Parliament passed a series of laws that deprived those unwilling to accept the new settlement of Church of England of the right to hold office, to attend Oxford or Cambridge, or to assemble for open worship. The various elements of the puritan movement reconstituted themselves as separate denominations—principally Congregationalists, Presbyterians, Baptists—while more radical faiths that had arisen, such as the Quakers, also organized as separate bodies. Nonconformity still had an influence on the nation's politics and culture, however, and the following decades saw some of the major puritan contributions to literature, including

John Milton's *Paradise Lost* (1667) and John Bunyan's *The Pilgrim's Progress* (1678).

New England puritanism was also threatened by the Restoration. The puritan colonies had supported Parliament and Oliver Cromwell in their efforts to erect a kingdom of God in England. The colonists had stopped swearing loyalty to Charles I and asserted their allegiance to Parliament. They had appointed days of fast and prayer to ask God to intercede on behalf of the puritan cause in England. Perhaps as many as a third of the colonists returned to their motherland in the 1640s and 1650s; some served in the army, some in government positions, others in the reforming church. John Cotton had preached a sermon justifying the regicide. He and other colonists who remained in New England had been major contributors to the outpouring of books exploring the subjects of how England's church and state should be reformed. The colonies had profited from their close connection to the puritan regimes, gaining exemption from England's Navigation Acts and receiving military support against a threat from the Dutch in New Netherlands. There was little reason to expect that Charles II would look favorably upon them.

During the 1660s and 1670s the English government engaged in a series of steps to curtail and undermine the powers of the puritan colonial governments. The colonies were prohibited from using extreme methods of punishing dissent (particularly the execution of Quakers). A royal commission was dispatched to investigate the ways in which the colonists had exceeded their legitimate powers. The colonists were ordered to no longer limit the franchise to church members and to open Communion in their churches to all Christians. New Englanders resisted such demands, but their refusals were themselves taken as additional transgressions. The churches of the region divided over a proposal, known as the Half-Way Covenant, which was intended to modify the standards for church membership. The colonists also faced growing challenges to their godly kingdoms from within. New immigrants, who had little sympathy with the puritan way of life, were drawn to Massachusetts and her sister colonies by economic opportunities. The growing prosperity of the region led to many youth adopting fashions and practices that were deemed excessive and sinful by their elders.

Led by John Eliot, New Englanders in the 1640s had embarked on an effort to convert and civilize the Native population. Eliot translated the Bible and other texts into the regional Algonquin language. Land was allocated for Praying Towns in which Native converts could live in the English style, govern themselves, and worship as Christians. By 1675 there were more than a dozen such communities and over fifteen hundred Christian Indians. But the very success of the English in drawing Natives away from their tribes and culture was a growing source of tension in the region. The continuing physical expansion of the English settlements meant the loss of Indian lands and the decline of the tribes' ability to sustain themselves. In 1675 the Wampanoag sachem Metacom (King Philip to the English) led a broad-based assault on the English settlements. King Philip's War was devastating to the English—more than a dozen towns were destroyed, about 10 percent of the white population were casualties—and even more catastrophic to the Natives. Many New Englanders saw the war as punishment from God for having violated their covenant promises to him. Clergymen such as Increase Mather preached jeremiads—a traditional sermon form that pointed to declension and urged spiritual renewal—to call for a reformation of manners.

King Philip's War so weakened New England that it was inconceivable that the colonists could have effectively resisted a determined thrust by the royal government to bring the region under control. In 1684 the English courts revoked the Massachusetts Bay charter. Following the death of Charles II in 1685, his brother and successor James II created a Dominion of New England, which over the next two years incorporated all of the region's colonies plus New York and New Jersey into a single colony with a royal appointed Governor General and no elected legislative body. Efforts were taken to introduce the Prayer Book worship of the Church of England, which the first colonists had left England to escape. Land grants were called into question, and the rights of town meetings restricted. All of this reflected the autocratic views of the Stuart monarchs, particularly James II.

Opposition to James, who was a Roman Catholic, grew following the birth of a son and heir, an event all suspected would lead to continuing Catholic rule. In 1688 this concern was a key element in the Glorious Revolution, which placed the Dutch ruler William of Orange and his wife Mary Stuart on the English throne as joint monarchs. In New England, a rebellion in Boston in April 1689 toppled the Dominion, and in 1691 King William allowed the various colonies to resume their separate identities (with the exception of Plymouth, which was incorporated into Massachusetts). A new Massachusetts charter restored an elected lower house of a bicameral legislature but made the office of governor a royal appointment.

The puritan effort to create a godly kingdom in America, which began with John Winthrop in 1630, had developed as one that relied on the colonists' virtual political autonomy to shape the character of their city on a hill. While the new charter restored some of the puritan settlers' ability to influence government policy, they no longer exercised political authority. Future puritans would have to impact their society through informal measures such as the creation of voluntary associations formed to advance religious goals.

The actions that would most seriously tarnish the historical reputation of the New England puritans, the Salem witchcraft episode of 1692, occurred after the collapse of puritan political control. The proceedings against accused witches were instigated by puritans, and the court that adjudicated the charges was comprised of puritans. It was a dark note that even more than their

3. This reconstruction of the Danvers, Massachusetts, meetinghouse demonstrates the simple style preferred by New Englanders for church services and town meetings. It was here that the first examinations of the Salem witches were held.

loss of government power signaled the end of the puritan era in America.

Belief in witchcraft was universal in the early modern world, part of a worldview that perceived the devil as a malevolent force that could both possess and afflict men as well as women. Unexplained phenomena such as the death of livestock, human disease, and hideous fits suffered by young and old suggested the agency of the devil or someone in league with the devil—a witch. The same system of belief included folk techniques to tell fortunes, discover lost property, heal the sick, and ward off witches. The puritans who first settled New England had been familiar with possession, affliction, and exorcisms in England.

Witch hunts were common throughout Europe in the sixteenth and seventeenth centuries, with thousands of women and men being accused of being Satan's agents and executed. England's

Lancashire region had been a scene of witch hunts in the decades before the puritan emigration to America, and more than two hundred witches were ferreted out by Matthew Hopkins, the "Witchfinder General" in East Anglia, in the 1640s. Witches were prosecuted in virtually all of the English colonies in America in the colonial period. Given this background, it is surprising how few individuals were accused and convicted of witchcraft in New England prior to 1692; there were only sixty-one known prosecutions in the region and at most sixteen convictions, four of those following confessions. Fewer than one in five who proclaimed their innocence were found guilty.

The Salem episode began with the observation of frightening symptoms experienced by a handful of girls and young women in an already bitterly contentious rural community outside of the town of Salem. The failure of the community's physician to find a medical explanation for their affliction led many to conclude that the devil was at work. Like other residents of Massachusetts, the people of the village were troubled by fears of Indian attacks on the frontier, the recent political upheavals, and uncertainty about the colony's future. Further uncertainty about the legitimacy of the colony's interim government inhibited the quick legal disposition of charges. When the newly appointed royal governor William Phipps arrived, the jails were already full of accused men and women awaiting trial. Phipps appointed a special court to hear and judge the accusations. The chief judge, William Stoughton, chose to accept as valid a type of testimony—spectral evidence—that had not previously been allowed in New England witchcraft trials and was generally condemned by all authorities on the subject. Before calmer heads prevailed on Governor Phipps to bring the proceedings to a halt, fourteen women and five men had been hanged as witches.

Having begun as a movement to transform individuals, communities, and nations through words and example, puritanism achieved political power in the seventeenth century in both

England and New England. Their experiments to reshape society by imposing a set of beliefs and practices on citizens forced puritans to confront issues that they had not previously had to consider, leading to new considerations about their faith and lifestyle. The effort to impose reform failed. But in England and America, puritans and puritanism did shape attitudes toward personal responsibility, the individual's participation in government, and the importance of education that continue to define our culture.

Chapter 3
The puritan and his God

Like other religious faiths, the core of puritanism was an understanding of God and the individual's relationship to God. The starting point for puritan theology was a realization that attempting to understand the supernatural was, as St. Paul expressed it, to look through a glass darkly. Even without accounting for the effects of original sin, natural minds could not understand the supernatural, which by definition was beyond their experience. As the English clergyman Richard Sibbes wrote, it was possible to apprehend God but not to comprehend him. Nevertheless, some knowledge was possible. The creation revealed aspects of the creator. History suggested the designs of providence. But the most important source for understanding the supernatural was the Scriptures, the direct revelation of God to men. And some men and women might have their understanding enhanced by an apprehension of the divine presence in their own lives.

The particular beliefs of the puritans were rooted in the Protestant understanding of the broad Christian tradition. Many of their theological positions were shared by men and women who would not necessarily be called puritans. Like virtually all of their contemporaries, puritans had no doubt that God existed, that men sinned, and that there was an afterlife in which some enjoyed heaven and others suffered in hell.

Unbelief was not an option for the men and women of the sixteenth and seventeenth centuries. Furthermore, despite their best efforts to reach agreement on the essentials of faith, puritans were no more capable of achieving a total uniformity of belief than most Christian groups. No scholar would argue that all puritans subscribed to a single, coherent orthodoxy that can be labeled "puritanism." Nevertheless, most of those labeled puritans were united in a common understanding of the nature of God, the sinfulness of man, and the relationship between divinity and humanity. And all rooted their beliefs on the Bible, which they saw as the revealed word of God.

God

Puritans had no doubt that God existed, the proof being found in the evidence of creation, in scripture, and in the apprehension of his presence in their own lives. Toward the end of the seventeenth century, in response to the stirrings of the Enlightenment, some theologians such as Richard Baxter and John Howe began to rely more heavily on natural theology, on the new understanding of nature as proof of God's existence.

All puritans believed that God, like other aspects of the supernatural order, was fundamentally incomprehensible. God could be fully understood only by God, but certain attributes of the divinity could be grasped. Like most Christians of their time, puritans believed that God was an eternal, immutable Spirit, infinite in goodness, power, wisdom, justice, and all other things. The single Godhead consisted of three distinct and coequal persons. How this could be so was one of the mysteries of faith, accepted as true by believers but incapable of being fully comprehended by natural reason. The three-in-one concept of the Trinity referred to the Father, the Son, and the Holy Spirit, and puritan authors would stoutly defend this view against heresies such as Arianism or Socinianism that suggested that Christ was created by God and not coeternally part of the Godhead.

The challenge for all men and women of faith who have a particular revelation of the essence of God is the difficulty of explaining to others something totally beyond their experience. The eighteenth-century New England clergyman Jonathan Edwards described this plight as the equivalent of describing the taste of honey to someone born without a sense of taste, or describing a rainbow to a person born blind. Puritans often spoke of God by drawing analogies to man's experiences, employing terms that might be used of human agents, using masculine pronouns, and speaking as if divine decisions were made in the same way as human ones. But they recognized that such language risked limiting the understanding of God to a particular form. One reason for their opposition to painted, carved, or sculpted images of the deity was that such objects fixed in people's minds a specific and therefore limiting view of God. For instance, the common Christian image of God the Father as an elderly bearded white man risked detracting from what might be seen as the feminine qualities of the deity. Many puritans wrote and talked about the maternal attributes of God, one example being John Cotton, who titled his catechism for New England youth *Milk for Babes, Drawn Out of the Breasts of Both Testaments*, the Scriptures being the

Peter Sterry on God as Mother

Lay the mouth of your soul by faith to the breasts of the Godhead laid forth in Christ, swelling with all fullness; longing, delighting to be drawn, yea of their own accord spouting forth their milky streams into your face and bosom.

Source: The Peter Sterry MSS at Emmanuel College, quoted in N. I. Matar, "A Devotion to Jesus as Mother in Restoration Puritanism," *Journal of the United Church History Society* 4 (1989), 307.

means by which God bestowed a mother's love. The London artisan Nehemiah Wallington wrote of God coming to reassure him like a loving mother. In the second half of the seventeenth century, the clergyman Peter Sterry often spoke of Christ as the saint's mother.

Man

While reluctant to probe too deeply into the essence of God, puritans had a lot to say about the nature of man and the relationship between God and his creation. In the beginning, they asserted, God made humans, male and female, after his own image. They believed that God entered into a conditional promise—referred to by many as the Covenant of Works—with Adam and Eve, offering them eternal life and happiness in paradise in return for their perfect obedience to God's commands. The original sin of Adam and Eve had consequences not only for them but for all their posterity. As the *New England Primer* would instruct children learning their alphabet, "In Adam's Fall, We Sinned All." Puritans might disagree over the process whereby all who came into the world were tainted by this original sin, but they were united in their understanding of the consequences for Adam and Eve and for all men and women who came after them—physical suffering, illness, and death became part of the human condition; spiritually, human faculties were disoriented and the soul corrupted.

Man was created as a moral agent with free will. Born with their understanding corrupted by original sin, which was embedded in their nature, men and women would commit their own transgressions of God's law. On given occasions the individual chose to do that which was forbidden by the law, choosing what promised self-gratification rather than obeying the law of God. The specifics of that law had been spelled out in the Ten Commandments God had given to Moses. Men and women turned from God and sought gratification of their senses, though they would find that physical pleasure would not satisfy them. The commandments were laws, not suggestions, and because each man and woman violated the law, each deserved damnation, the punishment for sin. Nothing a person could do could break this bondage to sin—all men were, to use modern terms, not only sinners but addicted to sin. Nehemiah Wallington wrote in one of his notebooks his conviction that as long as he lived, sin must and would remain in him.

Robert Keayne on Good Works

I do further desire from my heart to renounce all confidence or expectation of merit in any of the best duties or services that I have, shall, or can be able to perform, acknowledging that all my righteousness, sanctification, and close walking with God, if it were or had been a thousand times more exact than ever yet I attained to, is all polluted and corrupt and falls short of commending me to God in point of my justification or helping forth my redemption or salvation. They deserve nothing at God's hand but hell and condemnation if he should enter into judgment with me for them. And though I believe that all my ways of holiness are of no use to me in point of justification, yet I believe they may not be neglected by me without great sin, but are ordained by God for me to walk in them carefully, in love to Him, in obedience to his Commandments. . . . They are good fruits and evidences of justification.

Source: Bernard Bailyn, ed., *The Apologia of Robert Keayne* (New York: Harper, 1964).

It was characteristic of puritans to subject themselves to intense self-examination as they sought to come to terms with their nature. Their belief in their sinfulness was verified by Scripture but rooted in self-awareness. They recorded their recognition of their darker impulses in diaries and conversion narratives. Men and women seeking admission to Thomas Shepard's church in Cambridge, Massachusetts, told of how they had come, with God's grace, to recognize their miserable estate, their vile nature, their barren hearts, acknowledging that they were filthy worms of creatures. Although they were humbled by this recognition and struggled to improve, they consistently fell back into sin. How could they be saved? Were they saved?

Predestination

Puritans followed the teachings of Augustine, Luther, and Calvin in stressing that giving man any role whatsoever in God's decision to offer salvation detracted from the omnipotence of the deity and was the rankest of errors. The implication of this was that at any time, some living men and women were destined to go to hell and others to heaven, *and nothing a person did could change this decree.* Unlike some modern cultures that espouse a faith in human perfection and offer second chances, puritans emphasized human fallibility. Indeed, they rejoiced in this teaching because they had come to accept their unworthiness. To use an imperfect analogy, they believed that they were living on death row, justly condemned for crimes they did commit. Yet the divine governor would pardon some of them, not because they had been convicted in error—they deserved the ultimate punishment—but because God was good and loving. Hope existed where there was no cause for hope. The point was not that God didn't save everyone; the point was that God need not have saved anyone.

The bare bones of the doctrine of predestination were clear. The specifics of how these decrees came about were less clear, and Calvin himself had discouraged too much inquiry into the ways of God on this matter. God was eternal—which did not mean that his existence began before creation and stretched into time without end, but that it was timeless. Applying human constructs of time and sequence to an eternal being was recognized as very problematic. Yet many Reformed theologians disregarded Calvin's

cautions and sought to probe deeply into the mind and actions of
the deity. They wanted to ask if the judgment of predestination
applied to only the elect, or if the damned were predestined to hell
before their birth (double predestination). Most said yes—after all,
the mind of God comprehended all things past, present, and
future. Pushing their inquiries even further, puritan theologians
such as William Perkins and John Preston debated such points as
whether the divine decrees were determined before or after Adam's
Fall, whether or not the sentence of damnation resulted from God's
foreknowledge of the sins the damned would commit, whether
Christ's sacrifice was sufficient for all but applied only to some, and
the means whereby Christ's sacrifice was made effectual in the lives
of those who were elect. While they condemned the contemporary
Dutch theologian Arminius for suggesting that man had to act
in accepting the offer of salvation, some skirted close to this in
their efforts to establish man's responsibility for his fate. Puritan
examinations of predestination's nuances occupied the thinking of
many theologians, but the doctrine was not elaborated in most of
the catechisms they wrote and used, and few parish clergymen
sought to explore the details of it in their weekly sermons.

Federal theology

Puritans often used contractual language such as the "Covenant of
Works" and the "Covenant of Grace" to make sense of the
relationship between God and man. Scholars have labeled their use
of such formulations to explain the process whereby the elect were
saved as the "Federal Theology." Developed among Reformed
theologians in the late sixteenth century, this theology was most
strongly articulated in England by puritan theologians such as
Dudley Fenner and William Perkins. The Covenant of Works
referred to the command and promise God gave Adam before the
Fall. If man obeyed the moral law as God commanded he would
merit salvation. By sinning, Adam and all men deserved
damnation. Christ's redemptive sacrifice on the cross made
possible the Covenant of Grace. Grace referred to God's favor and

mercy, which he gave freely to the elect. This superseded and abrogated the Covenant of Works for the elect.

In the early seventeenth century, theologians such as John Preston and John Cotton argued that God not only offered saving grace to the elect but gave them the ability to perform covenantal obligations of faith, repentance, and obedience. This understanding of the Covenant of Grace reduced or eliminated the individual's role in the process of salvation by emphasizing the sufficiency of God's work. These clergy and those who followed their lead tended to emphasize God's boundless love of the elect, comparing it to that between parent and child or husband and wife. In the later seventeenth century, theologians such as Thomas Goodwin underlined this concept of God's self-sufficiency by positing the notion of an eternal pact between Father, Son, and Holy Spirit, referred to as the Covenant of Redemption, whereby the salvation of the elect was determined and effected.

Applied theology

During the late sixteenth and early seventeenth centuries many puritan preachers sought to apply this theology to the concerns of their parishioners. They taught that all people were subject to the requirements of God's law. Drawn to sin, everyone at one time or another would choose to defy the commandments. Consequently, all men deserved God's punishment and deserved to be damned. Because of their fallen nature, no man or woman could merit salvation. This was a central tenet of puritan belief, confirmed by their observation of the behavior of others, but even more so by their awareness of the darker impulses of their own nature and their own actual sins against God's law. This awareness of his own inability to ever be worthy of salvation is what had led Luther to challenge the teachings of the Roman Catholic Church and deny the efficacy of works.

Yet puritan preachers and authors consoled their followers with the belief that God had shown himself to be benevolent as well as just. In his goodness he offered to some a second chance—the Covenant of Grace. Through the redemptive sacrifice of Jesus Christ, salvation was granted as a gift to men and women who had been selected by God. This was a free gift from God; a sinner could do nothing to move God to offer it to him, nor could he refuse it if offered. Theologically, this was the moment of justification, when the merits of Christ were applied to the individual soul. Some referred to this as a conversion, in which the individual was transformed from a sinner deserving death to one of the elect who was promised heaven.

God made his choice manifest in different ways to different people. The most dramatic story of an individual being saved through God's work on his soul was that of Saul, persecutor of Christians transformed into Paul on the road to Damascus. Some who experienced justification as such a dramatic transformation believed that they had been born again. While typically a puritan was a young adult when he or she experienced God's redeeming work, deathbed conversions were not unknown.

But conversion could also be a gradual, subtle process. The clergyman Thomas Goodwin suggested that most men were unaware of God's working in their souls, a troubled conscience being replaced by a sense of God's comforting presence, bringing confidence in one's election. Others thought that the elect were customarily drawn to God through a series of discernable steps. A common schema saw the process beginning with introspection, examination of the Scriptures, and listening to the preached word, all of which would prepare the individual to recognize his sinfulness and feel contrition for his sins. Contrition was followed by humiliation when the sinner came to terms with his inability to break away from sin. The individual recognized that he owed a debt to God that could not be repaid by any amount of good works.

Anne Bradstreet's Conversion

In my young years, about 6 or 7 as I take it, I began to make conscience of my ways, and what I knew was sinful, as lying, disobedience to parents, etc. I avoided it. If at any time I was overtaken with the like evils, it was as a great trouble, and I could not rest 'till by prayer I had confessed it unto God. I was also troubled at the neglect of private duties though too often tardy that way. I also found much comfort in reading the Scriptures, especially those places I thought most concerned my condition, and as I grew to have more understanding, so the more solace I took in them.... But as I grew to be about 14 or 15, I found my heart more carnal, and sitting loose from God, vanity and the follies of youth take hold of me. About 16, the Lord laid His hand sore upon me and smote me with the smallpox. When I was in my affliction, I besought the Lord and confessed my pride and vanity, and He was entreated of me and again restored me.

Source: Anne Bradstreet's letter to her children, in *The Works of Anne Bradstreet*, ed. Jeannie Hensley (Cambridge, MA: Harvard University Press, 1967).

Some puritans believed that most men and women could reach this stage of awareness.

Salvation, however, was possible only through God's mercy, which was bestowed only on the elect. At this point the person would experience justification, the infusion of God's saving grace, which announced the individual's salvation and rehabilitated his or her faculties. As noted, for some this experience was a dramatic transformation, which they referred to as being, in essence, born again. The result of this change was sanctification—the progressive growth in the saint's ability to better perceive and seek God's will, and thus to lead a holy life. But whether the transformation was sudden and unanticipated, or more gradual through discernable steps, the work of salvation was God's and not man's.

Assurance of God's love typically waxed and waned in those who believed themselves saved. Faced with doubts, many were reassured by a new experience of God's caress. The use of the sexual imagery from the Old Testament Song of Songs to describe Christ's embrace of the elect attests to the intensity of the experience felt by puritans such as Samuel Rogers. Other puritans relied on a meticulous process of spiritual bookkeeping and hoped to find reassurance in a record of leading a better life than before their first experience of grace—looking, in essence for the fruits of salvation in their behavior. In an effort to guide their followers toward understanding the nature of the exemplary lives the saints were called upon to live, puritan clergy in the late sixteenth and early seventeenth century produced a large number of spiritual guides. William Ames wrote that theology was the doctrine of living to God, and works of practical divinity became the hallmark of puritanism. Books such as Richard Rogers's *Seven Treatises* (1603), Richard Sibbes's *The Bruised Reed and Smoking Flax* (1630), Henry Scudder's *Christian's Daily Walk* (1627), and Arthur Dent's *The Plain Man's Pathway to Heaven* (1601) set out the details of personal and corporate piety, which the elect were urged to take advantage of in their journey to sanctification.

Though intended to offer pastoral help to believers, these works of practical divinity were perceived by some as borderline Arminianism because of their intense focus on works. Critics of this approach were likely to react by emphasizing purely subjective experience for assurance, making themselves vulnerable to the charge that they were drifting toward the total differentiation of salvation from works that was labeled Antinomianism. Given the desire to know if one was saved and the difficulty of achieving full assurance, many puritans vacillated between these two poles.

The climax of the elect's progress toward God was referred to as glorification, or heavenly blessedness. When the gates of the Celestial Kingdom opened for the Christian, then was assurance complete and final. Glorification removed all of the imperfections of soul and body that had been wrought by sin. The saint would have the beatific vision of God, glorify God forever, and enjoy his presence forever. While some, such as the New England clergyman Jonathan Mitchell, believed that the saints might experience the beginnings of glorification in their earthly lives, this view was not widely shared. Toward the end of the century, however, perhaps connected with the growing earthly trials of the puritan cause, writers such as John Bunyan and Richard Baxter began to direct their readers to contemplations of heaven and its rewards.

Providence and the devil

Puritans believed that the final outcome of the life of individuals and of mankind was preordained, and referred to the divine blueprint for human history as providence. The world was, indeed, the theater of God's judgment. Yet they also believed that en route to that end the way the story would unfold was influenced by man's free will and by the interposition of supernatural forces. The universe was not a machine that ran automatically according to an initial plan. God not only sustained the universe by the emanation of his power, but he was believed to intervene in natural affairs as a means of showing his favor to a person or group, or to send a message by punishing those who opposed his way. Venereal disease was commonly viewed as a judgment of God against those who had sinned sexually. The sudden death of an individual who had scoffed at a godly clergyman or at observance of the Sabbath was interpreted by puritans as a divine intervention to remind all men of the need to respect God's agents. In general, this belief offered reassurance that everything that happened occurred for a reason, even if that reason might not be readily apparent to men. These beliefs led to a close study of history (and a scrupulous recording of it) to detect signs of God's plan so that men and women might better work to advance it, and also to a close examination

A Providential Tale

In the edge of Essex near Brinkley, two fellows working in a chalk pit, the one was boasting to his fellow how he had angered his mistress with staying so late at their sports the last Sunday night, but he said he would anger her worse the next Sunday. He had no sooner said this, but suddenly the earth fell down upon him, and slew him outright, with the fall whereof his fellow's limb was broken, who had been partner with him in his jollity on the Lord's day, escaping with his life, that he might tell the truth, that God might be glorified, and that by this warning he might repent of his sin and reform such his profaneness, and remain as a pillar of salt, to season others with fear by his example.

Source: Henry Burton, *A Divine Tragedy Lately Acted* (1642).

of everyday events to determine if they occurred as messages from God.

On a broader level, providentialism contributed to the belief that certain peoples had been chosen by God for special roles in history. Many saw England as an "elect nation" called upon to lead the world to triumph over the papacy and the forces of Antichrist. Those who believed this pointed to events such as the defeat of the Spanish Armada and the discovery of the Gunpowder Plot as signs of God's special care for England. Some New Englanders saw their colonies as chosen to preserve and advance the gospel. John Winthrop told those who joined with him in the journey to New England that they would know that they were following God's will when ten colonists could overcome a thousand of their enemies, whoever those enemies might be.

Complicating this scrutiny of natural and historical occurrences was the belief that events could also be shaped by the power of the devil. Puritans believed that God allowed the devil to afflict individuals in material ways. Some saw lightning as fire hurled

4. Increase Mather (1639–1723), the leading clergyman of late-seventeenth-century Massachusetts, was author of *An Essay for the Recording of Illustrious Providence* (1684).

from the sky by devils. The devil could possess an unwary soul and live within that person to control his every word and action. The devil could also draw individuals to his service, tempting them with promises of power and pleasure as related in the story of Dr. Faustus as told by the playwright Christopher Marlowe. Those who succumbed to the temptation were witches, to whom the devil gave the ability to harm people and their livestock. But most puritans believed that they were most likely to encounter the devil as the tempter who urged them to seek their own good rather than God's, or who injected blasphemous thoughts into their minds, sowed the seeds of despair in their souls, or led them away from the moral life.

Chapter 4
Living the puritan life

Given that puritans believed that nothing they did could influence whether they would spend eternity with God in heaven or damned in hell, it is extraordinary that they devoted the attention they did to behaving in a godly fashion. The simple explanation is that they believed that God gave his law to be obeyed, and it was their duty to do so irrespective of any rewards they might receive. Puritans who believed that they were numbered among the elect further explained their ability to adhere to God's wishes by claiming that grace had made them more capable of perceiving God's will and more successful in carrying it out. But there were other reasons as well.

It was not unusual for the confidence of the born-again puritans to wane, their hearts feeling hollow. On such occasions, some were reassured by an experience that they described as God's caress. Nehemiah Wallington wrote of how he felt Jesus coming like a tender mother or father to draw the curtains of his bed, looking upon him, and taking Wallington to himself. John Winthrop spoke of being so ravished with Christ's love that he was filled with unspeakable joy. Wallington and Winthrop weren't alone in using sexual images to speak of God's love, and it was commonplace to talk and write about Christ as the soul's bridegroom. For some who experienced such spiritual ecstasy, no further validation of their election was needed.

Some puritans, however, never had this type of intense emotional experience. Because of the belief that those who were saved were sanctified, when such men and women experienced doubt they looked to their good behavior for reassurance, seeing it as the fruit of salvation, as evidence that they were indeed saved. Without denying their belief, this may well have set up a subconscious motivation for doing good. If one's life after the presumed conversion experience was qualitatively holier than life before, this would assuage one's doubts.

An exemplary life

Whether he or she received assurance from an immediate sense of God's presence or from the validation offered by a sanctified life, a puritan was committed to following the path of righteousness, to be (to paraphrase Thomas Goodwin) children of light walking in darkness. While perfection was impossible, one was called to strive for it. Each puritan sought to make him- or herself a shining light, a small kingdom of God that would inspire others to godly living. Yet what did it mean to live a godly life? How was sinfulness defined? Did puritanism make individuals joyless and repressed as the popular stereotype portrays them?

The clergyman Richard Baxter wrote that "overdoing is the ordinary way of undoing," and this is perhaps the best guide to understanding puritan morality. Puritans believed that all of creation was a gift of God and thus intrinsically good. Sin came not from using what God had made available, but from abusing it. And no matter how excellent something was, it could be overdone. At one point in New England the civil magistrates expressed their concern to the clergy that so many religious lectures were being delivered that the settlers were neglecting their material tasks. This effort to define a line between use and abuse can be demonstrated by examining three areas commonly misunderstood.

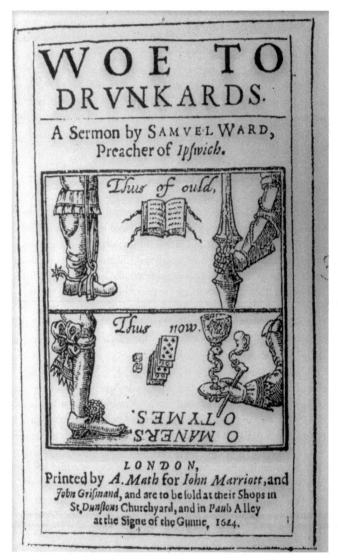

WOE TO DRVNKARDS.

A Sermon by SAMVEL WARD,
Preacher of *Ipſwich*.

Thus of ould,

Thus now.

O MANERS. O TYMES.

LONDON,
Printed by *A. Math* for *Iohn Marriott*, and
Iohn Griſmand, and are to be ſold at their Shops in
St. *Dunſtons* Churchyard, and in *Pauls* Alley
at the Signe of the Gunne, 1624.

5. *Woe to Drunkards*, a tract by Samuel Ward of Ipswich, England,
pointed to some of the sins of the time criticized by the puritans.

Puritans viewed drunkenness as a sin; drinking was acceptable. Indeed, this was an age when most of what Englishmen drank to quench their thirst had an alcoholic content. Water was contaminated by human and animal waste, making it a beverage of last resort. Milk too carried health risks in an age before pasteurization. Coffee, tea, and chocolate drinks were just making their way into European consciousness. So for Englishmen, beers, ales, and stouts were the beverages of choice for adults. "Small beer"—a less potent brew—was offered to children who had been weaned from their mother's breasts.

Contrary to the way in which they have often been depicted, puritans did not all dress in drab-colored clothing. Keenly aware of social status, like their contemporaries, puritans believed that men and women should appropriately dress for their station in life. Laborers dressed in woolens dyed in earth tones because such clothing was durable and less likely to show dust and dirt. Puritans of a higher status could wear class-appropriate dress; inventories show that men and women owned outfits of silk and satins in a variety of bright colors. Magistrates and ministers were likely to have clothing dyed black, but this was a sign of their distinction since black was the most expensive fabric to make and a sign of high status, not sobriety. The clergyman William Perkins set out the theory when he wrote that apparel for the scholar, the tradesman, the farmer, the gentleman, and all others should be appropriate to the individual's station in life. However, puritans did reject fashions such as bodices cut excessively low and exaggerated male codpieces, both of which they believed were sexually provocative. Deciding how many ribbons on a dress were excessive or how many fashionable slashes should be allowed on the sleeve of a gentleman's outer shirt was contested within communities.

Sexuality is another area in which puritans were not "puritanical" as normally understood. Traditional Christian values were based on the notion that celibacy was a superior moral state and that sexual acts of any sort involved gratification of sexual desires that

6. Anne Pollard (1621–1725) arrived in Massachusetts in the first years of settlement and lived through the Puritan era in New England.

could easily become sinful. Many medieval churchmen cautioned that while sex within marriage was allowed (and necessary) for procreation, engaging in sex frequently, or for the purpose of enjoyment, was sinful. This was changing in the Reformation era, a major shift occurring when Luther rejected the idea of clerical celibacy and embraced marriage as the normal state of life for a Christian. While procreation was still seen as an important function of marriage, greater emphasis was placed on the importance of the union in providing companionship and support. Intercourse between husband and wife was encouraged not simply as a means for having children, but as a joyous expression of love that bound the couple together. This new emphasis potentially opened the door for dissolving marriages if the couple proved incompatible, a position strongly advanced by the poet and polemicist John Milton, though most of his fellow puritans rejected the idea.

Puritans were among those who advanced these new views on marriage and sex. While clearly some men and women in puritan societies still held to traditional positions, clergy could be heard reminding their parishioners of the "duty to desire." The minister William Gouge wrote that intercourse between man and wife was to be conducted willingly, often, and cheerfully. A Massachusetts man was excommunicated by the Boston church for withholding sexual favors from his wife. The letters of John Winthrop and his wife Margaret reveal their physical yearning for one another when they were apart. The New England poet Anne Bradstreet referred to her husband Simon as her missing sun, whose warmth melted the frigid colds of New England and whose heat gave them their children.

While intercourse between husband and wife was viewed by these men and women as the proper use of the sexual drives God gave

Anne Bradstreet to Her Husband

To My Dear and Loving Husband
If ever two were one, then surely we.
If ever man were loved by wife, then thee;
...
My love is such that rivers cannot quench,
Nor ought but love from thee, give recompense.
Thy love is such I can no way repay,
The heavens reward thee manifold, I pray.
Then while we live, in love let's so persevere
That when we live no more, we may live forever.

Source: Anne Bradstreet's letter to her children, in *The Works of Anne Bradstreet*, ed. Jeannie Hensley (Cambridge, MA: Harvard University Press, 1967).

them, any other form of sexual activity was viewed as an abuse. Puritans condemned fornication, adultery, homosexuality, bestiality, and other sexual indulgences outside of marriage. Such temptations were to be fought, and the London puritan Nehemiah Wallington reminded himself that one who even looked on a woman with lust had committed adultery with her in his heart. But such condemnation was the reverse side of a celebration of marital sex, a celebration underlined by the comparisons puritans drew between the joy experienced in union with Christ and the joy of sexual love between husband and wife. Clearly, this was a comparison that would not have been made if puritans viewed sexuality as sinful. As in the use of drink, attire, and other such parts of the creation, the puritan's attitude toward sex has been misinterpreted.

The daily discipline

The clergy urged puritans to subject themselves to a daily discipline designed to assist them in making proper choices as they sought to serve God and their neighbors. The scholar Perry Miller identified "Augustinian Piety" as one of the hallmarks of puritanism, and advice manuals and diaries are replete with evidence of this approach to life. Puritans believed that the day should begin with a private time to pray and reflect upon one's life. Nehemiah Wallington, who had a tendency to excess, often rose as early as four o'clock in the morning (and sometimes earlier) to pray and meditate. He wrote that these sessions on occasion brought him a sense of spiritual sweetness and a sense of God's presence with him that prepared him for the day to come. On one occasion he felt that through his meditation he entered into a corner of heaven. For Wallington and some other puritans, this was also a time to commit their self-reflections to a diary, which they would consult in later times as a means of charting their spiritual progress.

Morning spiritual exercises were also a time to renew a commitment to living a Christian life in the day to come. Clergymen urged believers to take time in the day to pray, and to read Scripture. They urged that time also be found to read works of practical divinity such as Richard Rogers's *Seven Treatises* that would help shape the believers' lives. The individual was to reflect on the sins he was especially prone to commit so that he might guard against those urges. A puritan was to dedicate himself to helping others, especially fellow saints. At the end of the day he was to reflect on his behavior, asking himself how well he had fulfilled his daily duties.

Directions for Daily Living

1. That we keep a narrow watch over our hearts, words, and deeds continually.
2. That with all care the time be redeemed, which hath been idly, carelessly, and unprofitably spent.
3. That once in the day at the least, private prayer and meditation (if it may) be used.
5. That our family be with diligence and regard, instructed, watched over and governed.
7. That we stir ourselves up to liberality to God's Saints.
8. That we give not the least bridle to wandering lusts and affections.
10. That we bestow sometime not only in mourning for our own sins, but also for the sins of the time and age wherein we live.
14. That we read somewhat daily of the Holy Scriptures.

Source: Richard Rogers, *Seven Treatises Containing Such Direction as Is Gathered Out of the Holy Scriptures* (1610).

Worldly callings

Just as the puritans believed that they had received a religious calling from God, so too they believed that they had been fitted by the creator with talents and skills that determined their earthly vocations. While medieval theologians had asserted that each person's social and economic station was determined by God, puritans sacralized secular vocations by arguing that part of the individual's duty to God was to use those gifts effectively in the tasks to which they had been called. Some callings were more complex and rewarding than others—John Winthrop believed that it was part of the divine plan that some would be rich and others poor; that some would be powerful in state and society and others live in humble circumstances—but each person was equally important to the needs of the social body. Winthrop was clear to point out that differences in one's calling did not represent differences in the quality of the person, and the English theologian William Perkins likewise asserted that all callings were equal in the eyes of God—the master of the house and the housekeeper, the landlord and the shepherd. Both these puritans warned that none should be looked down upon because of his or her calling, and that while society might bestow more power on some men than others because of their particular calling, all men should be treated with equal respect.

The critical point for puritan teachings was that no matter what one was called to do, the call came from God. One was not merely fitted by the deity to be, say, a carpenter—one was obliged to respect those gifts by being the best carpenter one could be. This teaching could certainly energize individuals to be productive, and this is what led the sociologist Max Weber to connect puritanism with the spirit of capitalism. But what Weber neglected to take sufficient account of was that as in their teachings on the moral life, puritans believed that the pursuit of one's calling could be excessive. If an individual focused on his business to the point where he neglected his obligations to his family, his church, or his community he sinned.

Robert Keayne was a merchant who regularly gadded about London to hear and take notes on the sermons of the leading puritan clergy. He migrated to Massachusetts in the 1630s and soon became an active member of the Boston church and a prominent member of the community. But in the eyes of his peers, Keayne behaved inappropriately when he charged what were seen as excessive prices for the goods he sold. Censured by his congregation, Keayne was humiliated but took steps to correct his practices, and in his will donated funds for the erection of a Town House in Boston. Nevertheless, he struggled with where the line existed between marketplace behavior that was allowable and that which was not. Keayne was troubled by the fear that he was too devoted to his economic interest. Nehemiah Wallington erred in the opposite direction. He devoted so much time to sermon gadding (up to nineteen in one week) and other religious exercises that he struggled to support his family.

Leisure

Puritans were not pleasure-hating, but they did try to place leisure and recreational activities within the framework of how they viewed the moral life. They believed that there was a proper place for leisure, which they saw as necessary to refresh and strengthen the individual, enabling him to return more effectively to the pursuit of his earthly and spiritual tasks. Distinctions, however, were to be made between appropriate and inappropriate forms of recreation, and some of these choices set them apart from their contemporaries. Much of the antipuritanism of the time was rooted in the perception that the godly sought to suppress the traditional pastimes of Merry England.

Puritans favored recreation that took them into the countryside. Boston's Samuel Sewall took his wife berrypicking and his family on picnics on one of the islands in Boston harbor. Fishing was another recreation commended by clerical authors as truly relaxing and devoid of temptations. Women as well as men were encouraged to fish. Hunting was more controversial. While John Winthrop hunted fowl in his native Suffolk, he was criticized by local puritans when he hunted in southeast Essex. In New England, where hunting was not primarily recreational but provided an important supplement to the family food supply, objections to the practice seem never to have been raised.

Blood sports such as bearbaiting and cockfighting were universally condemned by puritans and criticized by some Englishmen who were not puritans. While opponents denounced activities (such as betting) associated with these "sports," their principal objection rested upon the sin involved in inflicting injury on God's creatures for sport. Similar concerns led puritans to oppose boxing.

Ball games met with a mixed response. Puritans almost universally condemned football, which at the time had few rules and pitted village against village in bloody, limb-breaking violence. Some clergy advised against tennis, which they associated with the Catholic monks who had played the game in monastic courtyards, but in fact Cambridge colleges, including the most puritan of all, Emmanuel, had tennis courts for the recreation of their members. Bowling likewise was suspect in the eyes of some, for many were prone to bet on the outcome. Governor William Bradford recorded that there was bowling in early Plymouth colony—he objected to the fact that some of the colonists (having begged off work on Christmas) were bowling instead of working or praying, but not that bowling occurred in the settlement. By the mid-century, nine-pin bowling had become an accepted pastime in the colonies.

The period that saw the rise of puritanism also witnessed the rise of the theater, culminating in the performance of works by William Shakespeare, Christopher Marlowe, and Ben Johnson. Although the puritan city fathers of Coventry commissioned a religious play on the "Destruction of Jerusalem" in the 1580s, and though plays were performed in some Oxford and Cambridge colleges and some puritans clearly adapted theatrical techniques to their preaching, puritans generally condemned the theater. William Prynne's *Histrio-Mastix* (1633) was perhaps the most vehement attack. The reasons offered by Prynne and other writers were numerous. Some cited the deceit intrinsic in the presentation of fictional tales; others objected to the actors, who were unruly. Still others argued that plays inspired depravity, and there is no doubt that the south side of the Thames, where London's theaters were located, was also a center of prostitution. The performance of plays on the Sabbath was a particular complaint. While many municipal officials who were not puritan shared these concerns, they seemed unable to curtail the abuses. Under the Puritan regime of the 1640s and 1650s theaters were shut down. In New England there was no performance of plays while the puritans retained control of the government.

The Plymouth episode recorded by Governor Bradford underlines the fact that for puritans even legitimate recreation was inappropriate in certain circumstances. One of the events that had alienated puritans from King James I was the proclamation (referred to as the Book of Sports) that he first ordered read from all pulpits in 1617. The proclamation permitted people to indulge in what it referred to as honest and healthy entertainments on the Sabbath. While some of the permitted activities, such as the raising of Maypoles, were condemned under any circumstances, others were objected to only if they were indulged in on the Sabbath, which puritans sought to maintain as a day for purely religious observance.

The situational aspect of puritan morality also dictated their views of music. Despite persistent myths, puritans were not opposed to music. They objected to choral music and the use of musical instruments in church services because they believed that these were remnants of Roman Catholicism that diverted parishioners from the proper focus of the services. Psalm singing was considered appropriate as a part of worship, though writers differed on how best the congregation was to be involved. Puritans did enjoy music in their homes, seeing it as a way of bringing the family together, and many men and women played instruments.

Some music was performed at the court of Oliver Cromwell in the 1650s, and the Lord Protector is said to have encouraged opera.

Like music, puritans accepted the legitimacy of dancing in some contexts and not others. Mixed dancing involving men and women was condemned as often leading to fornication, a concern that was based as much on observation of communal revels in England as on theory. Increase Mather was quick to find scriptural and historical authorities to condemn what he called "promiscuous dancing" when a dancing school was opened in Boston following the loss of the Massachusetts charter. Forms of folk dancing that did not involve close contact between the sexes was, however, generally accepted by puritans.

Social gatherings that involved feasting, telling stories, and sharing news were forms of recreation embraced by puritans. They regularly gathered with friends and neighbors for parties, to commemorate the ordination of a new clergyman, to work together in raising the town's meetinghouse or a townsman's barn, and or to celebrate weddings and baptisms. Smaller gatherings of friends might feature singing or card-playing, which most puritans found acceptable, if wagering was not involved.

In their efforts to regulate personal and communal morality the puritans sought to make themselves, their families, and their neighborhoods godly kingdoms whose light would shine forth and provide an example for others seeking to properly serve God. In setting upon this course as intensely as they did, they developed a distinctive character that set them apart from many of their fellow Englishmen, who in turn subjected them to ridicule and abuse.

Chapter 5

The puritan and his neighbors

Anne Bradstreet wrote that "as a man is called the little world, so his heart may be called the little commonwealth." Each individual was to shape his life in accord with the will of God so that he or she could become a shining light, a model of faith that would inspire others. Having first brought his personal life under the rule of God, the puritan then strove to influence a progressive transformation whereby his family would become a godly realm, his parish a godly parish, and then the society as a whole a godly kingdom. Much of what puritans wrote concerning society can be found in the works of other writers as well, but the intensity with which they pursued these ideals was what had led friends to call them godly and enemies to disdain them as precisionists.

The family

The foundation of larger puritan communities was the family. As Bradstreet referred to the individual as a little commonwealth, so the London clergyman William Gouge was one of many who used the term to refer to the family. John Cotton talked of a family covenant of mutual obligations that bound the members of the family to one another. Within this small society, each member had a role. The foundation of the family was the relationship between husband and wife. Puritan teachings sought to create a balance between traditional social teachings that emphasized the

61

TENTH MUSE

Lately ſprung up in AMERICA.

OR

Severall Poems, compiled
with great variety of VVit
and Learning, full of delight.

Wherein eſpecially is contained a com-
pleat diſcourſe and deſcription of

The Four
- Elements,
- Conſtitutions,
- Ages of Man,
- Seaſons of the Year.

Together with an Exact Epitomie of
the Four Monarchies, viz.

The
- Aſſyrian,
- Perſian,
- Grecian,
- Roman.

Alſo a Dialogue between Old England and
New, concerning the late troubles.

With divers other pleaſant and ſerious Poems.

By a Gentlewoman in thoſe parts.

Printed at London for Stephen Bowtell at the ſigne of the
Bible in Popes Head-Alley. 1650.

7. *The Tenth Muse*, Anne Bradstreet's book of verse, was the first
published work by an American woman.

hierarchical structure of the family, their belief in the importance of each individual's personal relationship to God, and the new emphasis on the companionable nature of marriage. While not all puritans lived up to these ideals, the insights that the records allow us into marriages such as that of John and Margaret Winthrop, Simon and Anne Bradstreet, and Samuel and Hannah Sewall are striking for the love and respect that bound these couples together.

Gouge acknowledged the traditional subordination of wives but tempered this when he stated that the husband ought to make his wife a joint governor of the family and delegate many aspects of family life to her direction. Furthermore, in the absence of their husbands, puritan wives such as Margaret Winthrop were expected to govern their little commonwealth in his place, administering the family business, instructing the young members of the household, and leading family prayer. Samuel Sewall worried that his pursuit of business and civic responsibilities may have led him to neglect his wife. Reflecting these concerns, in the puritan commonwealths erected in New England women were given greater legal protections than was customary in England.

Husbands and wives shared responsibility for supervising their children and the authority to govern them. Clergymen instructed fathers and mothers that their first duty as parents was to nurture and provide for their children. They were to feed and clothe them. They were to educate them. The Massachusetts General Court passed legislation requiring the heads of household to teach their children and servants how to read and write. It was essential for parents to instill in those children the same understanding of the faith and practice of piety that defined their own faith. They sought to break the sinful wills of their children, if necessary by physical correction, but more commonly by expressing their own sorrow for the harm that the child's sin had done, thus playing upon natural bonds of affection to stimulate a sense of guilt. Samuel Sewall recollected only one occasion when he had used physical punishment for one of his children. Again, there was no single rule, because, as Anne Bradstreet recognized, children differed from each other—some were like meat that needed the abrasive application of salt to prevent putrefaction, others tender fruit that needed to be preserved with sugar.

Family religious observances were an important means of achieving these ends. Roger Clap, one of the early settlers of Dorchester, Massachusetts, advised his children to worship God daily as a family, engaging in family prayer in both morning and evening, and reading Scripture to the gathered members of the family every day. The Sabbath was often a day of intense family piety. Woodcut illustrations showing the family gathered around the head of household as he instructed them in their catechism or read to them from the Bible were a staple in the manuals of piety published in this period. There is some indication that in the latter seventeenth century, when women were more likely to be

8. Family worship was a central feature of puritanism.

church members than men in both England and New England, mothers began to play the greater role in directing family religious piety. But indirect instruction was also called for, and puritan authors urged believers to be exemplars of faith and piety to their children.

There is no basis for saying that puritans were not emotionally attached to their children. Though they were resigned to the loss of a child, a common experience in this period, they did care deeply about their children. Increase Mather often sat up all night praying at the bedside of a sick child. Nehemiah Wallington was inconsolable for weeks after the death of his daughter from the plague in 1625.

Puritan discussions of the religious obligations of parents almost invariably addressed their roles as the heads of the entire household. This meant that servants and—in New England—slaves were included among those for whom parents were responsible. They were to be taught to read if they did not come to their service with this skill. They were to be catechized and included in family prayers and scripture reading. Because a servant's stay in a household was usually of short duration, puritans occasionally expressed frustration at the difficulties involved in fulfilling these obligations successfully.

The Sabbath

Puritan families were insistent upon proper observance of the Sabbath, and this was a matter where their intensity often created divisions in the local community. The fourth commandment mandated that the Lord's Day be kept holy. By the 1580s puritans had developed an understanding of the Sabbath that, while not unique to them, was identified with them. For the godly, the Sabbath began at sundown on Saturday and ended when the sun set on Sunday. This was a time for fasting, family religious exercises, and worship. Men and women were to avoid all but the most essential labor. Recreation was forbidden, which is what made the Book of Sports the flash point that it became.

Having prepared themselves by family prayer and meditation, the members of the puritan household assembled at church for public worship, many carrying Bibles and, in some cases, paper, pen, and ink to take notes. For the godly the centerpiece of weekly worship was the sermon: the preached word was not only a means to better understand their faith, but the means most often used by God to break a sinner's heart and prepare it for saving grace. Sitting in the pews, many of the godly took notes to review and discuss at a later time with fellow saints.

When it was offered, the Lord's Supper was also a source of nourishment. The Essex clergyman John Rogers referred to the word and the sacrament as the two breasts of the church. Despite its importance, the Lord's Supper was not an integral part of the regular worship of the Church of England in the way that it was for Catholics. In some English churches and in New England it was offered monthly. Because they valued the communion they experienced in this sacrament, puritans were insistent that only those properly prepared and at peace with their fellow congregants should be admitted to the table. Because of this concern and their belief that the sacrament only bestowed grace on those whom God had already touched with his saving caress, New Englanders decided that only those admitted to church membership should participate. English puritans who formed gathered churches (congregations formed by voluntary association rather than geography) in the 1640s and 1650s, or who restricted the sacraments to those parish members who swore to a church covenant, did likewise. By the end of the seventeenth century, however, clergy such as New England's Solomon Stoddard began to argue that the Lord's Supper, like the preached word, could be a converting ordinance, and advocated a more liberal admission policy.

Conferencing

While the family was quite literally the home for puritan religious observance and the church was the center for formal worship, godly men and women also derived support from social communion with fellow saints. John Cotton urged the saints to seek society with faithful friends, who could offer them strong support in times of trial. The English clergyman Richard Rogers urged believers to come together with other saints in formally organized covenanted groups that would meet regularly and aid their members in sustaining their faith. In his *Seven Treatises*, he offered an example of such a gathering that he had organized in Wethersfield, England. That model likely influenced John Winthrop, who organized a group of lay and clerical friends, women as well as men, that would formally meet once a year but would pray for each other every Friday. When they met, Winthrop wrote, they did not discuss knotty matters of theology but rather shared their personal religious experiences, which he found refreshed him and quickened his own spirituality. Some such groups were led by a parish clergyman and brought together the godly segment of a religious community for extra prayer and

A Community Covenants

In the year 1588 there met in a Christian man's house certain well minded persons, who dwelt in one town together, with whom also the preacher of the place did meet at the same time. Their meeting was for the continuance of love, and for the edifying of one another, after some bodily repast and refreshing.... This meeting was a great whetting them on to enjoy the public ministry more cheerfully and fruitfully afterwards: and this means [a covenant] with others, both public and private, did knit them in that love.

Source: Richard Rogers, *Seven Treatises Containing Such Direction as Is Gathered Out of the Holy Scriptures* (1610).

discussion. Others, consisting only of laypeople, were separate from the church and a means of sustaining the faith where the local parish or parishes were insufficiently sympathetic to the concerns of the godly. Some conferences were limited to lay men, while in others women played a key role—such as those involving Brigit Cooke in Kersey, England, and Anne Hutchinson in Boston, Massachusetts. Members of such groups shared religious books and manuscripts with each other in addition to joining in prayer and discussion. All of these gatherings, but particularly those separate from the parish church, were attacked by many bishops as conventicles that threatened the lines of proper authority in the national church, and it is true that some gatherings did lead to separatism.

These gatherings were vitally important in England, where even in the heavily puritan Stour Valley saints were confronted by many who disdained their views. But even in New England, an overwhelmingly puritan society, these conferences played an important role. Roxbury, Massachusetts, pastor John Eliot described how in some of the private meetings in the colonies believers prayed, sang psalms, repeated sermons, and shared their individual experience of God. At times, he claimed, the members felt that they were virtually in heaven.

Conferences were voluntary gatherings, and as puritan laity and clergy strove to aid each other in furthering the common understanding they came to rely on the judgment of all those in whom they perceived what Oliver Cromwell called "the root of the matter" in them. This was an essentially democratic tendency, which flourished in America as the polity of congregationalism that came to be known as the New England Way.

Parishes and congregations—the New England Way

Not all puritans were Congregationalists, asserting the autonomy of the individual congregation in determining its affairs. Some would have been content with a reformed episcopacy, willing to accept a national church with bishops if those leaders fostered reform and shared responsibility with local churches. Others looked to Scotland for a Presbyterian model of church government, where elected classes or presbyteries exercised authority over individual congregations. But in the place where puritanism became most established, New England, the participatory polity of Congregationalism was chosen. There the saints formed churches from nothing. A meeting of the community identified a small group of particularly godly men (usually including one who had been ordained in England) to serve as the pillars of their church. These men drafted a formal covenant in which they pledged to join in the proper worship of God and to nourish each other in the search for further religious truth. They then extended invitations to others in the community to join them in swearing to the covenant, admitting as members those who had an understanding of the faith and also a reputation for godliness. Once the initial composition of the congregation had been set, the members chose two clergymen, a pastor and a teacher, to minister to them, and lay elders to manage the nonspiritual affairs of the church. While all members of the community were required to attend services, only those admitted to the church as members could avail themselves of the two sacraments administered in New England, the Lord's Supper and Baptism.

Critics accused the colonists of following the path of separatism, but the New Englanders insisted that they still considered themselves part of the communion of the English Church. There were various precedents other than separatist practice which they drew on, including the exiles on the continent who had organized their own churches in communities in Switzerland and the Netherlands. Some English parishes had the right to choose their own clergy. Henry Jacob had organized an independent congregation in London along lines similar to the New England Way.

A Church Covenant

The 15 articles and covenant of Mr. Hugh Peter of Rotterdam 1633:

2. To cleave in heart to the true and pure worship of God, and to oppose all ways of innovation and corruption.... 4. To labor for growth of knowledge and to that end to confer, pray, hear, and meditate. 5. To submit to brotherly admonition and censure without envy or anger.... 9. To further the Gospel at home and abroad as well in our persons as with our purses.... 11. To take nearly to heart our brethren's condition and to conform ourselves to these troublesome times both in diet and apparel that they be without excess in necessity. 12. To deal with all kind of wisdom and gentleness towards those that are without. 13. To study amity and brotherly love.... 15. for the furthering of the kingdom of Christ, diligently to instruct children & servants, yea, and to look to our ways and accounts daily.

Source: British Library, Add. MS. 6394: The Boswell Papers. Part 1, f154.

Each New England congregation was an independent entity, and from church to church there were variations in the balance of lay authority and clerical influence, how high the bar was set for admission to membership, and other matters. To preserve the general uniformity of the churches, the ministers met regularly just as English clergy had. On occasion synods (or assemblies) with lay and clerical representatives were called to address matters of importance—two examples were the Synod of 1637, which identified errors that were being advanced during the controversy that swirled around Anne Hutchinson; another was the Cambridge Assembly, which developed the formal statement of New England orthodoxy in 1649. But congregationalism dictated that synods could only make recommendations; the ultimate decision to accept or reject them was that of the individual congregation.

The dynamics of congregational interaction varied from place to place, and changed over time. Some clergy expected to be deferred to by the members of their church—Thomas Hooker's Hartford colleague Samuel Stone at one point described the New England Way as characterized by a preaching aristocracy (the pastor and teacher) and a silent democracy. Yet there is clear evidence that in some congregations lay involvement in church affairs was active and vocal. Over the course of the seventeenth century the clergy as a group began to perceive of themselves as members of a profession who should exercise greater power within their congregations, and in some parts of New England sought to organize institutionalized clerical assemblies that would have authority over individual churches. At the same time, laymen became more willing to challenge the leadership of their pastors, a trend that came to the fore when numerous congregations rejected their clerical leaders' advice about whether their own congregation should accept the expansion of baptismal practices recommended by the Synod of 1662. Contributing somewhat to both of these trends was the fact that in contrast to the experience of the first generation, whose clergy had often been part of the immigrant group that called them to the ministry, second-generation clergy were Harvard graduates likely to have had no prior contact with the congregation that called them. Change also led to the growth of different factions within the lay membership, so that whereas most congregational decisions in the early history of New England were only confirmed when there was unanimous consent, in the second half of the century majority rule was the best that could be achieved on some issues.

Parishes and congregations—English experiments

For English puritans the opportunity to begin the reform of the national church that they long sought came during the 1640s. The nature of their task was significantly different from that faced by New Englanders. The colonists had been writing on a clean slate, creating pure churches in a New World. For their English co-religionists the challenge was how to reform a national church containing large numbers of members who saw no need for the reforms the puritans were seeking.

Puritanism as a movement had never committed itself to a particular form of church government as divinely sanctioned, and that was still true at the start of the English Civil Wars. The Westminster Assembly appointed by parliament to recommend reforms proposed the transformation of the national church into a Presbyterian system: each parish would have its own presbytery; parishes were to be supervised by local classical presbyteries, with a hierarchical structure reaching up to provincial and national assemblies. The Long Parliament did seek to implement these recommendations by passing legislation calling for the election of parish elders and the division of London's parishes into twelve classical presbyteries, but they did little else to implement the plan, referring it instead to local authorities. Proposals from various localities led to the creation of various forms of Presbyterian government in Lancashire, Derbyshire, and other regions, but no two were exactly alike, and there was never a national assembly convened as envisaged in the original proposal.

Those clergy who supported the plan for a Presbyterian church ministered to parishes as well as they were able but were frustrated by the Parliament's failure to establish the supervisory system that the plan required. Some advocates of the New England Way accepted parish livings (often the same ones they had left in the 1630s) and initially carried on as puritan parish clergy always had, though seeking over time to limit the sacraments to those parishioners who were judged saints and covenanted together. This was, for instance, what John Phillip attempted when he returned from New England to once again serve as rector of Wrentham, Suffolk. Both of these groups of clergymen showed a strong traditional commitment to the parish ideal.

During the 1640s and 1650s other puritans chose to abandon parishes in which saints mixed with sinners and formed their own congregations with members from different parishes coming together. This was particularly true of those who rejected infant baptism or were adherents of other nonorthodox views. But some of these gathered churches were attempts to create New England–style churches of saints independent of any hierarchical authority. Samuel Eaton was successful in this in Cheshire. An important distinction is that whereas parish clergy were still supported by tithes, gathered churches were required to support their clergy from their own resources. What emerged was a patchwork of parishes and congregations with little consistency—individuals and churches that agreed on forms of ecclesiastical government might disagree on theology and practices, while those who agreed on faith and ceremonies might disagree over whether Presbyterianism or some form of Independency was desirable. Adding to the complexity was the rise of lay preachers and their supporters who rejected the need for a university trained ministry and gathered their own congregations.

In the aftermath of the Restoration, most puritan clergy found it impossible to remain within the Church of England, although some, such as Ralph Josselin and John Angier, did manage to retain their parish livings without wearing vestments or conducting worship as prescribed by the Book of Common Prayer. For the first time, however, other puritans began to organize as distinct denominational groups defined by a particular view of church government (Presbyterians and Congregationalists) or distinctive beliefs (Baptists). These groups came to be known collectively as Nonconformists or Dissenters. The hope that had once burned for a uniform puritan England had died. In the process puritans had come to redefine their understanding of the proper relationship between church and state.

Chapter 6
Puritans and the larger society

Aligning themselves, their families, and their friends with God's will was preliminary to the puritan goal of reshaping the world around them. Their view of the proper society was that of a living organism in which each person had his or her distinct but complementary role. John Winthrop spoke of society as a body and its members as the various parts that were to be bound together by the ligaments of Christian love. In an age when many were crafting a philosophy of individualism, Puritans generally asserted the importance of community and bending private aspirations to societal needs. In doing so they were not being original but drawing on a medieval heritage that many other Englishmen adhered to, particularly the tradition of Christian Republicanism that was influential in Elizabethan times.

Perimeter fences

In defining itself, every society determines a set of core values, which all citizens are expected to abide by. In doing so its members establish what one scholar has called a perimeter fence, the boundary between people and ideas that are acceptable and those that threaten the existence of the society and are not to be tolerated. Such a boundary is reinforced by the process whereby some are excluded from the group and others voluntarily set themselves apart from it. Where the definition of what is acceptable is informal (as opposed to being mandated by law), the line may be vague and imprecise. This was the case during the Elizabethan period in England. For much of that time puritan efforts were focused on the common Roman Catholic enemy and issues that distinguished the godly from their fellow English Protestants were not that pronounced. By the time James I ascended the throne, the domestic Catholic threat, while still of concern, had receded in importance. Puritan clergy such as Arthur Dent directed their primary focus to the men and women in their parishes who were nominally Christian but deemed by the godly to be insufficiently zealous. This coincided with the developing emphasis of practical divinity on defining the nature of proper religious observance and godly living.

Puritans in the early seventeenth century called for stricter observance of the Sabbath, raised their voices against theater and blood sports, and urged the importance of family devotions and godly conferencing. In drawing a sharper distinction between the godly life and that of the ungodly, these clergy produced a counterreaction from those who were unwilling to deny themselves traditional social activities and pleasures. While there were some earlier examples of antipuritan polemic, it was in this period that attacks on puritanism gained strength. Over sixty plays satirized puritans as killjoy moralists or hypocrites who were often sensualists. They were faulted as wild enthusiasts on the one hand and for promoting excessively long and deadly dull prayers and sermons on the other. Among the most notable examples was Ben Jonson's character "Zeal-of-the-Land Busy" in *Bartholomew Fair* (1614). Various figures in the works of William Shakespeare have been identified as representing negative images of puritans. Many of these portrayals would be seized upon in later centuries by critics of the puritan tradition.

How much such images affected relations between men and women in England's parishes is open to question. Public criticism of a perceived religious enemy did not necessarily turn members of a local community against one another. In areas where the godly were a minority, puritans were likely to be subjected to abuse. In response, they erected a perimeter fence to clearly distinguish themselves from the ungodly and sought to have as little as possible to do with those neighbors. In areas such as the Stour Valley, long a puritan stronghold, the boundary between the godly and their nonpuritan neighbors was not as significant. However, the effort of Charles II and bishops such as Richard Neile and William Laud to institutionally define the line between accepted belief and practice and nonconformity changed the religious dialogue throughout the nation.

Prior to the establishment of what may be called the puritan regimes in New England in the 1630s and in England in the 1640s, puritans were forced to advance their agenda by words and example. Power gave the godly the opportunity to institutionally define acceptable belief, church practices, and moral behavior, and to impose that definition of godliness on all who lived under their authority. They feared that God might punish them if they failed to punish those who defied his wishes.

Pursuing the millennium?

In the twentieth chapter of the book of Revelation the Apostle John writes of a thousand-year rule of the saints on earth with Christ. As careful students of Scripture, it was to be expected that puritans would seek to understand their role, if any, in the events there foretold. Many tied the millennium to the prophecy in the book of Daniel, which predicted that after four earthly monarchies were overthrown, a fifth, godly kingdom would be erected—a kingdom some equated with the rule of the saints prophesied in Revelation. Most believed that the conversion of the Jews to Christianity would precede the climax of these events. While recent scholarship suggests that many earlier writers overstated the millennial element in mainstream puritanism on both sides of the Atlantic, the presence of such thinking cannot be denied. The fierce anti-Catholic stance of puritans contributed to their interest in the final, apocalyptic struggle between Christ and Antichrist. The magnitude of the Thirty Years War had prompted speculation that it was the climatic struggle between the forces of Christ and Antichrist, and the settlement of New England and the outbreak of England's Puritan Revolution led others to inquire as to the providential meaning of those events and the role that they were to play in the coming of the millennium.

Some New Englanders saw their enterprise as the creation of a New Jerusalem, though not the physical center of the millennial kingdom. The quest for purity of worship was reinforced by millennial beliefs. John Eliot and others believed that the Native Americans were the lost tribes of Israel and saw their missionary efforts as bringing about the conversion of the Jews foretold in Revelation. John Cotton encouraged Oliver Cromwell in his attack on Spanish America because of his interpretation of that scriptural book. Those who advocated the strict adoption of the Mosaic code in the colonies did so, in part at least, because they believed that in turning back to those ancient ways they would bring their society closer to the millennium.

The Puritan Revolution (1642–60) fanned the fires of millennial expectation in England. Many of the sermons that puritan clergy preached to the Long Parliament drew on millennial rhetoric. Opposing and then executing the king was justified as part of God's plan to establish his kingdom on earth. The move to readmit the Jews to England was another consequence of millenarian beliefs. For those who saw their goal as establishment of the Fifth Monarchy and the direct rule of King Jesus, the Protectorate of Oliver Cromwell was little better than the rule of King Charles. Few puritans went as far as the Fifth Monarchists, but the attempt to bring themselves closer to the thousand-year rule of the saints did influence how puritans ordered their societies and their churches. The Restoration in 1660 changed the nature of English millennial writing but did not put an end to such speculation.

While few believed that they were literally ushering in the millennium, puritans on both sides of the Atlantic nevertheless saw themselves as having a role to play in bringing that end closer. New Englanders felt a more pronounced responsibility to create a godly society than their counterparts in England during the puritan ascendancy of the 1640s and 1650s. This was because the American puritan colonies were new creations, founded to be a godly kingdom according to puritan principles. For them, the goal could be achieved by regulating those allowed to live in their Bible Commonwealths. During the Free Grace Controversy that swirled around Anne Hutchinson, the Massachusetts General Court passed a law requiring that newcomers had to be approved by the magistrates before they would be allowed to settle. John Winthrop defended this law in an exchange with the former governor Henry Vane, arguing that a society has the right to exclude those whose views would be harmful to it. Nathaniel Ward made the same point in *The Simple Cobbler of Agawam* (1647) when he stated that those who disagreed with what New England stood for were indeed free—free to live elsewhere.

England's situation in the 1640s was different for a number of reasons. In the first place, puritans acknowledged that it was one

Winthrop on the Right of a Society to Limit Immigration

If we here be a corporation established by free consent, if the place of cohabitation be our own, then no man hath right to come into us without our consent.... If we are bound to keep off whatsoever appears to tend to our ruin or damage, then we may lawfully refuse to receive such whose dispositions suit not with ours and whose society we know will be hurtful to us, and therefore it is lawful to take knowledge of all men before we receive them.

Source: Allyn B. Forbes, ed., *Winthrop Papers, Volume III: 1631–1637* (Boston: Massachusetts Historical Society, 1943).

thing to insist on uniformity in a new society, but quite a different matter to impose a new order on a people that had lived by different beliefs for many generations. Furthermore, in their effort to achieve the primary goal of defending their rights against Charles I, puritans had been willing to call upon men of unorthodox religious views (such as Anabaptists) who were nevertheless committed to fight in the Parliamentary armies. Once the wars were won it was no easy thing to reduce everyone to a single orthodoxy. Thus English puritans were forced to tolerate a broader range of views and practice than their New England brethren, though they continued to labor through the 1650s to persuade all Englishmen of what they perceived as the truth.

Reordering society

Once in control of the agencies of authority, puritans used this power to attempt to impose a culture of discipline on the societies they governed and to insure that their puritan states would promote and protect true religion. The former task was easier in New England because settlers there were inclined to accept puritan cultural values, at least during the early decades of settlement. Thus there were no sports or other recreations on the Sabbath. Holydays such as Christmas were not celebrated. No theaters were allowed to open, and no one attempted to start a dancing school until the end of the seventeenth century. Maypoles were not tolerated. Alehouses were carefully regulated. Brothels were unheard of for most of the seventeenth century. Marriage was made a civil ceremony, and traditional religious ceremonies connected with death and burial were dispensed with, although private observances of such events were allowed. Magistrates punished drunkenness, fornication, swearing, and other moral excesses with the approbation of most members of the community.

In England the imposition of such measures was more contested. Theaters were closed and the celebration of Christmas banned, but not without opposition. Because not all local magistrates could be counted on to enforce such ordinances and to regulate moral behavior, the Protectorate appointed military commanders to administer ten districts into which England was divided. While these Major-Generals were responsible for discovering plots against the regime and maintaining civil order, they were also charged with promoting godliness. They were to suppress prohibited sports such as bearbaiting and cockfighting, close illegal alehouses and houses of ill repute, prosecute gambling, prevent swearing, and generally enforce a culture of discipline. They were also to assist in examining candidates for parish livings. While their tasks were little different from those of New England's magistrates, their success was limited by popular opposition.

Church and state

England, like most European countries in the early modern period, was characterized by a firm institutional connection between church and state. Not only was the king the supreme head of the Church of England, but bishops were members of the House of Lords (the upper house of Parliament) and sat as members of county Commissions of the Peace. In addition, leading clergymen, such as William Laud, were often to be found on the king's Privy Council and holding other important positions in the secular government. The law required membership in the national church, and those who recused themselves from its worship—Catholics and Protestant Separatists alike—were subject to civil penalties.

In both New England and Oliver Cromwell's England the state was looked upon as a guardian of faith, but efforts were made to create a greater than normal institutional separation. There were limits to this. Within a short time of the settlement of Massachusetts, the General Court decided that only those who were admitted as church members should be eligible for the franchise—though at the time that decision was made a personal conversion narrative was not required for membership. Nevertheless, in the colonies no clergyman could hold secular office. While clergymen (as university graduates and thus the colony's intelligentsia) were often consulted on public policy, their advice was not always accepted. If church proceedings sentenced a freeman to excommunication, that judgment had no impact on his civil right to vote; banishment by the civil authorities did not affect one's church status (though clearly participation in the congregation would be difficult). While the magistrates called on the churches to meet to decide on matters that threatened the peace of the churches, they did not seek to impose the recommendations of such gatherings on the churches of the Bible Commonwealths. Thus, while they recommended the Half-Way Covenant that emerged from the Synod of 1662, they did not seek to require churches to adopt it. Efforts of some colonists to have Massachusetts adopt the Mosaic Law was rejected in favor of a law code largely derived from the principles of English Common Law— a Common Law that was itself rooted in Judeo-Christian values.

In rejecting the closer connection of state and church that they had found confining in England, the colonists took steps to redefine certain aspects of the traditional religious sphere. They denied that places of worship were in any way holy, so that the meetinghouses that they built accommodated both gatherings for worship and town meetings. They rejected the notion that marriage was a sacrament and made it a civil union. They rejected the notion that men should be buried in what others viewed as the consecrated ground of churchyards; colonists were buried in town graveyards (something not always evident to modern observers since churches often were built next to these burial grounds in later centuries).

However, the puritan colonists saw the state as nurturing the churches. Going back to England and sermons such as that preached by Samuel Ward to the Suffolk justices of the peace in 1618, the puritan ideal was cooperation between Joshua and Moses, the magistrates and the ministers. Elected by godly freemen, magistrates such as the Massachusetts Bay Colony's John Winthrop and John Endecott and New Haven's Theophilus Eaton brought a puritan outlook to their task. Because they viewed the civil and religious spheres as mutually supporting, they saw religious beliefs that threatened the churches as disruptive of public order and acted against the offenders. They did believe that they had the right and obligation to prohibit certain types of activities on the Sabbath.

The magistrates also legislated that the youth of the Bible Commonwealths should be educated, citing civil reasons as well as religious ones. Whereas in England at the time fewer than 30 percent of the population could read and write, the leaders of New England's puritan colonies sought universal literacy. A 1642 law in Massachusetts required that heads of household teach those in their charge—wives, children, and servants—basic skills in reading and writing, and stipulated the value of citizens being able to read and understand the colony's laws as well as the benefits of being able to read the Bible. A 1647 law went further in ordering that all towns of fifty or more households employ a teacher to instruct those who were not able to be effectively taught in the home, and towns of one hundred or more households employ a grammar school teacher to prepare boys with the talent for possible college education. While the latter law specifically sought to obstruct the wiles of that "old deluder Satan," it too had as a goal the raising of an educated citizenry. The chartering of Harvard College in 1636 was designed to prepare youth for service in state and church.

The relationship between church and state in puritan England was more complex. The failure of Parliament to establish a reformed church structure during the period of the Civil Wars meant that there was a de facto toleration of a broad range of Protestant views. This included not only the freedom for men—and women—to preach whatever they wished, but for printers to publish whatever they wished. In 1650 the Elizabethan laws, which had criminalized

Old Deluder Satan Law

"It being one chief project of the old deluder, Satan, to keep men from the knowledge of the Scriptures, ... [so that] learning may not be buried in the grave of our fathers in the church and commonwealth, the Lord assisting our endeavors, It is therefore ordered, that every township in this jurisdiction, after the Lord hath increased your number to 50 householders, shall then forthwith appoint one within their town to teach all such children as shall resort to him to write & read, whose wages shall be paid either by the parents or masters of such children, or by the inhabitants in general ... as the major part of ... the town shall appoint. It is further ordered, that where any town shall increase to the number of 100 families or householders, they shall set up a grammar school, the master thereof being able to instruct youth so far as they shall be fitted for the university."

Source: Nathaniel B. Shurtleff, ed., *Records of the Governor and Company of Governor and Colony of the Massachusetts Bay in New England, 1628–1686* (Boston: Commonwealth of Massachusetts, 1853–54).

nonattendance at worship, were repealed. Tithes, however, though controversial, were still to be paid to the parish clergy. Shortly thereafter, under the Commonwealth and then the Protectorate, some efforts were made to set a perimeter fence.

A Blasphemy Act in 1650 set penalties for advocating certain extreme views, but efforts to produce a more precise statement of fundamentals of faith consistently broke down because of disagreements between those who were willing to allow little room within the perimeter fence for dissent and those who were willing to be more tolerant. In 1654 a commission of Triers was created, which was to approve the orthodoxy of those being considered for parish livings. The thirty-eight commission members were largely Congregationalists, with some Presbyterians and a few Calvinist Baptists. A separate group of local commissions of Ejectors was also established to judge clergy and schoolmasters who were accused of being ignorant, scandalous, or too heretical, and to eject from their livings those who were deemed insufficient. The government did not provide the Triers or the Ejectors with a doctrinal standard to apply, though the orthodox Calvinist outlook of their members certainly influenced the decisions. Major-Generals were to secure order, promote godly morality, and assist the Ejectors in their efforts, but the experiment was abandoned after two years, in part because of its unpopularity.

The limits of toleration

When John Winthrop shared his hopes for the New England puritan experiment in his "Model of Christian Charity," he expressed the hope that if the colonists dedicated themselves to leading exemplary lives, God would reward them by giving them a greater understanding of his truth than they had previously had. For Winthrop and other puritans who were humbled by awareness that they were sinners who did not deserve God's gift of election, perfection in life and belief was something to strive for but never achieve. They clearly identified certain ideas and practices as offensive to God, but they believed that communion and discussion with other saints could help all achieve a better understanding of God's will. Other puritans believed that God's grace enabled them to correctly discern what was acceptable and what was not, and sought to impose their certainties on all. Individuals such as the clergyman Thomas Shepard and the magistrate Thomas Dudley were likely to be more authoritarian and more intolerant of any ideas that differed from their understanding. Both of these men tended to use harsh, combative language in discussing those who challenged their understanding of the truth.

There were many religious debates in early Massachusetts, and many of them—such as that over whether the Roman Catholic Church was a true church despite its errors—were settled without fragmenting the religious community. Indeed, the whole purpose of informal clerical conferences was to reach agreement when they could and to defer judgment on matters on which they remained divided. Less common, but more famous, were the differences that could not be peacefully reconciled, and they reveal the intolerance of true believers on both sides of the conflicts.

From his first arrival in New England in 1631 Roger Williams was dissatisfied with the fact that the churches of Massachusetts refused to formally separate from the Church of England. Even the Separatists of Plymouth, where he ministered for a time, were insufficiently committed to further purifying their practices. Returning to Massachusetts, he settled in Salem and continued to advance ideas which the majority of the colonists considered dangerous to the stability of the colony and its relationship to the royal government. He questioned the authority of the king to have granted a charter that bestowed on the colonists lands of the Native Americans. He fanned concerns about the use of the red cross of St. George (the symbol of English national identity) in the flags used by the colonial militia, probably leading the magistrate John Endecott to deface the colors by cutting the cross from the flag used by the Salem troops. He denied the right of civil government to stipulate Sabbath observance and to administer any form of oath (which he viewed as a religious act). When the magistrates and other churches sought to influence Salem to curb his enthusiasm, Williams demanded that the Salem congregation cut off all relations with the rest of the churches. In 1635 the General Court, led by Thomas Dudley, ordered Williams shipped back to England. Warned by John Winthrop, who remained his friend, he fled the Bay's jurisdiction and established the town of Providence. Over the following decades he continued searching for further understanding of God's ways, briefly adopting Baptist views, and finally concluding that there could be no true churches until Christ came again to create them. On each step of his religious evolution Williams obstinately insisted on the correctness of his views and the errors of those who opposed him.

Even more controversial was the case that revolved around Anne Hutchinson and other members of the Boston church. It was in the congregations of New England that the puritan impulse to reform was nurtured; because of Boston's identification as the center of government and the membership of leading magistrates such as John Winthrop in the community's congregation, that church played a key role in the affairs of Massachusetts. Visitors who came to the town for meetings of the General Court attended services at the church. Men and women from neighboring villages came to hear John Cotton's weekday lectures. In the early 1630s the church was a center of enthusiastic religious dialogue and shared experiences, the vitality of which was fueled by the constant flow of new immigrants from England, where puritans were increasingly under siege. Among those who joined it in the mid-1630s were the Hutchinson family, the Dyer family, and Henry Vane, the young and zealous son of one of the king's privy councilors. Within the congregation and in private lay conferences in the town a variety of ideas seem to have been aired and explored, including the role of immediate grace in salvation, the fate of the body after death, the nature of the Trinity, and other difficult matters of faith.

Not everyone approved of the open discussion of such ideas. Across the Charles River from Boston, in Newtown, Thomas Shepard was a proponent of a narrowly defined and strictly enforced orthodoxy, and throughout the colony others agreed with him that limits had to be placed on congregational explorations of matters they believed were settled. In 1636 Shepard challenged John Cotton for what he viewed as the airing of heretical views within Cotton's Boston congregation. Anne Hutchinson became the symbol of all of the views that Shepard deemed dangerous.

The controversy that evolved was a debate over where to draw the perimeter fence between orthodox views and unacceptable opinions. The colony quickly became polarized, with the supporters of Shepard attacking the enthusiasts as Antinomians who would substitute private urgings of the Spirit for the moral law, and Hutchinson and her supporters accusing all of the region's clergy, save Cotton and her brother-in-law John Wheelwright, as preaching a covenant of works that deluded people into thinking they could save themselves. On a fast day called to heal divisions, Wheelwright preached an inflammatory sermon in which he urged his supporters to fight (with spiritual weapons) against the anti-Christian forces that preached and supported false doctrine. The dispute had ramifications for civil order. Not only was it vital for any new colonial society to maintain order, but in this particular case supporters of the Hutchinson faction refused to serve against the Pequots because Boston's other clergyman, John Wilson, had been appointed chaplain of the forces.

The General Court charged Wheelwright with sedition and gave him time to reconsider his position. When many Bostonians challenged the actions of the Court, they were ordered to be disarmed. Because Wheelwright refused to compromise, he was banished, as were those of his supporters who refused to retract their challenges to the court. Anne Hutchinson was then brought to trial for fomenting much of the disorder. After ably defending herself against charges of having broken any laws, she claimed that it had been revealed to her that if the authorities acted against her, God would bring down ruin on them and their posterity. She too was banished. In a subsequent trial in the Boston church she was excommunicated for her persistently expressing views the majority of the congregation had by then agreed were outside the pale of acceptable doctrine. But the victory of Shepard and his supporters was incomplete. The ability of Winthrop, John Davenport, and others to build a moderate middle ground saved John Cotton and perhaps others from scrutiny that might have led to their own banishment. The perimeter fence was drawn more closely but not tightened as much as some wished.

As in the case of most religious disputes of this period, no one—not Roger Williams, Anne Hutchinson, nor anyone else—was

Anne Hutchinson to the Massachusetts Magistrates at her trial

Therefore take heed what you go about to do unto me, for you have no power over my body, neither can you do me any harm, for I am in the hands of the eternal Jehovah, my Savior. I am at his appointment. The bounds of my habitation are cast in heaven. No more do I esteem of any mortal man than creatures in his hand. I fear none but the great Jehovah, which hath foretold me of these things, and I do verily believe that he will deliver me out of your hands. Therefore, take heed how you proceed against me, for I know that for this you go about to do to me, God will ruin you and your posterity, and this whole state.

Source: David D. Hall, ed., *The Antinomian Controversy, 1636–1638* (Middletown, CT: Wesleyan University Press, 1968).

advocating a twentieth-century style pluralism that suspends judgment as to whether one religious viewpoint is more true than another. These dissenters were totally convinced that they were right and that the majority was, in essence, hell bent. Had they been willing to keep their views to themselves they would not have been expelled, but they (as much as those who banished them) viewed silence and acquiescence as a violation of their responsibility to God to speak out against what they viewed as error.

Over the remainder of the seventeenth century New England magistrates would engage with other religious groups, and the more conservative elements in the society would continue their efforts to exclude those whose views were deemed dangerously heretical. They were less successful in preventing the formation of a Baptist church, in part because of the colonist's own conflicted views on who should be baptized, and in part because of colonial awareness of the role played by university-trained Calvinist Baptist clergymen in furthering the kingdom of God in England at the time. Efforts to limit the proselytization of Baptist views was somewhat successful, but by the 1670s there was a Baptist congregation worshipping in Boston.

Quakers posed a greater challenge. They were far more confrontational in challenging the orthodox puritans and were unwilling to accept sentences of banishment, often returning to renew their efforts. Whipping did little to diminish their enthusiasm. Massachusetts passed legislation imposing the death penalty on Quakers who returned a second time from banishment and in 1659 hung two Quaker men while sparing Mary Dyer (who had once been a follower of Anne Hutchinson). She too was hanged in 1660 when she returned yet again. By this time some colonists were questioning the efficacy of turning Quakers into martyrs, but that debate was closed when Charles II forbade any future executions.

While circumstances in England resulted in a far broader tolerance of various religious views, there was a similar debate there between

Mary Dyer's Letter to the Massachusetts Magistrates from Prison

If you neither hear nor obey the Lord nor his servants, yet will he send more of his servants among you, so that your end shall be frustrated.... Oh! Let none of you put this day far from you, which verily in the light of the Lord I see approaching, even to many in and about Boston, which is the bitterest and darkest professing place.... In Love and in the spirit of meekness, I again beseech you, for I have no enmity to the persons of any; but you shall know, that God will not be mocked, but what you sow, that you shall reap from him, that will render to everyone according to the deeds done in the body, whether good or evil.

Source: Massachusetts Archives.

those who wanted to allow dialogue between a broader range of views and those who favored a more restricted freedom. Indeed, among the latter were many, primarily Presbyterians, whose desire to define and impose a narrow orthodoxy differed little from the most conservative New Englanders. But power was largely in the hands of Oliver Cromwell, and he was clearly among the former group, intolerant only of those who were themselves intolerant, recognizing different forms of godliness, and willing to learn from a variety of individuals, including the Quaker leader George Foxe. Yet while he was Lord Protector he accepted the decision to imprison John Biddle for publishing anti-Trinitarian views, he acquiesced in the execution and dismemberment of a Catholic priest, John Southworth, who had returned from banishment, and he was unable to mitigate Parliament's decision to have the Quaker James Nayler mutilated and imprisoned for blasphemy.

Oliver Cromwell on Religious Toleration

22 January 1655

Is there not yet upon the spirit of men a strange itch? Nothing will satisfy them, unless they can put their finger upon their brethren's consciences, to pinch them there.... Is it ingenuous to ask liberty, and not to give it? What greater hypocrisy than for those who were oppressed by the bishops to become the greatest oppressors themselves as soon as their yoke was removed?

Source: Ivan Roots, ed., *Speeches of Oliver Cromwell* (London: Dent, 1989).

Attention to how English puritans dealt with divisions within their ranks and with more radical forms of Protestant dissent should not obscure the fact that the Church of England as structured since the days of Henry VIII was uprooted. There was no place for bishops in the English puritan state, and countless parish ministers who clung to the old ways were ejected from their livings. Many men and women were attached to the Prayer Book forms and were as

displeased with the new puritan order in the nation and its
parishes as the puritans themselves had been opposed to the
Laudian order.

Intolerance of dissenting voices was characteristic of the age, when
most Christians were convinced that there was one religious truth
and that God expected them to defend it and thus protect his sheep
from error. It also remains one of the aspects of puritan history
that have rightly been criticized by latter generations. Eventually,
puritans in both Englands would lose the power to coerce those
who disagreed with them. After 1660 in England and following the
loss of the Massachusetts charter in 1684, puritans once again were
forced to rely on persuasion by word and example to spread their
message, as their ancestors had during the reigns of Elizabeth and
James I.

Puritans and others

It was not only other religious groups that puritans found
themselves engaged with on both sides of the Atlantic. To a great
extent men and women in the early modern era tended to define
themselves by reference to other peoples and cultures. In New
England, that process of self-identification centered on cultural
character. Native Americans were seen as a people apart not
because of their race but because they lacked the civilized behavior
and Christian faith of the puritans. In the first years of colonization
there was little contact with the Indians in Massachusetts since
most of the tribes of that region had been wiped out as a result of
diseases contracted from European fishermen and fur traders who
had sailed the coast since the sixteenth century. The expansion of
settlement brought the puritans into greater contact with various
native groups, one result being the Pequot War.

That conflict notwithstanding, it was essential to the English self-
image that they treat the native population in accord with their
own superior standards. New Englanders punished colonists who

transgressed against natives according to the same English legal procedures they used in judging their fellow settlers. They also accorded natives the protections of colonial law. In taking these steps, they were asserting the superiority of their culture. It never occurred to them to ask whether justice as they knew it accorded with native values.

If natives adopted English civilization and faith they were admitted inside the perimeter fence. By the 1670s more than fifteen hundred natives had adopted Christianity and settled in so-called Praying Towns where they adopted English social customs. One spur to these efforts was the belief of some that the natives were descendants of the lost tribes of Israel and that their conversion would be one of the steps foretold in the book of Revelation that would usher in the millennial kingdom. These efforts were supported by generous financial contributions from Englishmen. One convert, John Sassamon, aided Eliot in the translation of the Bible into the Algonquin language. Sassamon spent some time at Harvard College and became an intermediary between the English and his own people until he was killed, most likely by Wampanoag warriors, in the prelude to King Philip's War.

That conflict tested the confidence of the colonists in how much their missionary successes could be relied upon. The colonists could not comprehend how those successes and their territorial expansion had threatened native existence, and so could only view the uprising as treachery. Many colonists decided that no Indians could be trusted. Natives were attacked without provocation. Praying Indians were interned on Deer Island in Boston Harbor. Eventually, as their losses mounted, the colonial authorities allowed natives to serve in their forces as scouts and auxiliaries. But despite the contributions these Christian Indians made to the defeat of King Philip, the suspicions engendered by the war never went away. In a fundamental way, most New Englanders came

MAMUSSE

WUNNEETUPANATAMWE

UP-BIBLUM GOD

NANEESWE

NUKKONE TESTAMENT

KAH WONK

WUSKU TESTAMENT·

Ne quoſhkinnumuk naſhpe Wuttinneumoh *CHRIST*
noh aſoowesit

JOHN ELIOT.

Nahohtôeu ontchetôe Printeuœmuk,

CAMBRIDGE.
Printeuœp naſhpe *Samuel Green.* MDCLXXXV.

9. *Up-Biblum*, the Bible translated into the native language by John
Eliot, was published in Cambridge, Massachusetts.

thereafter to see natives as a race apart, with no place for them within the perimeter fence.

Over the course of the seventeenth century the English colonists were also forced to define the place of Africans in New England. There were a few blacks in Massachusetts before the arrival of the puritans, including at least three African slaves owned by Samuel Maverick on the peninsula that would come to be known as Boston. During the 1630s trade with the puritan colony of Providence Island brought a small number of other African slaves to Massachusetts, including some exchanged for native captives after the Pequot War.

What slavery meant for blacks in early New England is hard to determine, an issue clouded by the fact that in the 1630s some white colonists were "reduced to slavery" for crimes, and in the 1650s some prisoners from Oliver Cromwell's victories over the Scots were sent to New England as slaves. It does appear that culture was at least as meaningful as race in determining the treatment of blacks. They were to be instructed to read and write as were other members of the household, and they were expected to attend church services. At least one such slave met the high standards for full membership in the Dorchester, Massachusetts, church. In the eighteenth century a Society of Negroes was organized in Boston as a conference of godly slaves who read Scripture, prayed, and sang psalms together. Cotton Mather would rely on his African slave Omesius to help shape an experiment with inoculation as a way of preventing smallpox. Later in the century a black slave in a Boston puritan household, Phillis Wheatley, would become America's second published female poet. None of this, of course, can mitigate the fact that blacks were forcibly reduced to slavery and denied basic rights. Samuel Sewall made these points in his printed attack on the institution, *The Selling of Joseph* (1700), but his arguments failed to persuade his fellow puritans.

Puritans in England had their own encounters with others. The native Irish were looked down upon both as uncivilized and savage, and for their adherence to Roman Catholicism. When they rebelled in 1641, Englishmen were quick to accept the most inflammatory reports on the massacre of Protestant settlers. While the brutality of Oliver Cromwell's troops following their capture of the Irish towns of Drogheda and Wexford in the process of finally suppressing the revolt in 1649 was not uncommon in European warfare of the day, the actions were in part justified by Cromwell by reference to the savagery of the Irish earlier in the decade.

In a different vein, as Lord Protector, Cromwell engaged in dialogue with the Dutch Jewish leader Manasseh ben Israel and took steps to allow the readmission of the Jews to England, from which they had long been banned. This was in part, perhaps, a reflection of Cromwell's own interest in diverse forms of godliness but also motivated by economic concerns and the same belief in the need to convert the Jews that had spurred interest in the native tribes of America.

In their encounters with religious others, the puritans of England and New England were over time pushed toward a reluctant embrace of voluntary as opposed to state-mandated religious commitments and a degree of religious toleration. In the case of their encounter with those of different ethnic and racial backgrounds, the path they followed led toward greater suspicion and hostility.

In England puritans lost power in 1660; in New England the seizure of the Massachusetts Bay charter in 1684 led to a similar loss of political control. As had been the case in the sixteenth and early seventeenth centuries, puritans were once again forced to rely on informal means of persuading their neighbors and countrymen of their beliefs about God, the obligations to lead a normal life, the nature of family, the obligation to serve others, the value of education, and the proper ordering of communities. Over time those who had once been called puritans divided among various denominational identities, and then divided yet again. On the occasion of the 350th anniversary of the New England puritan Cambridge Platform, representatives of the United Church of Christ, the Unitarian Universalist Association, the national Association of Congregational Christian Churches, and the Conservative Congregational Christian Conference gathered to celebrate that foundational document and lay claim to that piece of puritan history. In England a similar broad spectrum of religious groups identify themselves with the puritan past. Within these churches, but in the broader societies as well, a puritan tradition and legacy have influenced English and American history long after there ceased to be men and women whom we would classify as "puritans."

Chapter 7
The puritan legacy

Over the course of the centuries during which the puritan movement became a puritan legacy, Englishmen and Americans have vigorously debated its influence. Some have praised their contributions; others have seen their legacy in negative terms. Few have doubted that the puritans played a major role in the evolution of those societies. The story of how puritans have been understood and misunderstood has itself become part of the meaning of puritanism.

England looks at its puritan legacy

It was in England that puritanism began, and in England that its dream of transforming the nation into a godly kingdom first was abandoned following the Restoration of the Stuart monarchy in 1660. While puritan clergy such as Richard Baxter and Thomas Goodwin continued to preach and write in an effort to persuade others to their faith, the most significant contributions to the puritan legacy in the decades after the Restoration were to be found in literature. John Milton's great poetic epics *Paradise Lost* (1667), *Paradise Regained* (1671), and *Samson Agonistes* (1671) can be read as allegories of the attempt to create a godly kingdom in England and the struggle for personal spiritual growth. Spiritual growth was also the focus of John Bunyan's *Grace Abounding to the*

Chief of Sinners (1666) and *The Pilgrim's Progress* (1678) as well as his other works, which offered hope and guidance to American as well as English puritans. Isaac Watts conveyed the affective piety of puritanism to later generations in his *Hymns and Spiritual Songs* (1707).

To a large degree early historical works dealing with puritanism replicated the disputes of the past. This was especially true of the accounts written by those who had lived through the events. Charles II's advisor Edward Hyde, the Earl of Clarendon, signaled his point of view in the title of his multivolume history of the conflict he had lived through, the *History of the Rebellion and Civil Wars of England*, the first volume of which was published posthumously in 1702. Edmund Ludlow wrote his *Memoirs* from the perspective of one of the saints who participated in the struggle and saw it primarily in religious terms.

The patterns set early continued. Conservative supporters of England's Establishment (Tories) connected puritanism with innovation, disorder, and revolution. In his popular *History of England* (1754–61), David Hume depicted puritans as fanatics who under the guise of piety subverted the established order. Cromwell, in particular, was portrayed as a hypocritical fanatic. Rejection of the seventeenth-century reformers became more pronounced during the late eighteenth and early nineteenth centuries as England confronted the power of Revolutionary France. The support that some contemporary English Dissenters expressed for the ideas of American and French revolutionaries strengthened Establishment disapproval of England's puritan rebels.

English proponents of greater liberties (Whigs) occasionally expressed a more positive view of the revolutions of the seventeenth century. Catherine Macaulay's *The History of England from the Accession of James I to the Elevation of the House of Hanover* (1769) praised the efforts of the Long Parliament in defending English liberties and for its experiment in republicanism. But Macaulay and other Whig authors had little interest in puritan faith and focused on the political rather than the religious thought of leaders such as Ludlow, Milton, and Algernon Sidney. They were as likely as the Tories to criticize Cromwell for what they saw as his illegal assumption of power and tyrannical rule. Historians who were themselves religious Dissenters, such as Daniel Neal, did address the religious issues, but presented the puritans as paladins of liberty and harbingers of democracy. Many Dissenters, influenced by the Enlightenment, had moved toward a more rational theological position, which made them uncomfortable with the enthusiasm of early puritanism. Neal accepted that religious uniformity could not be achieved and that all parties in power in England had been guilty of persecution.

The repeal of the Test and Corporation Acts in 1828 broke the established Church's monopoly on power and began the fuller integration of Dissenters (and Catholics as well) into English life. This, as well as a period of stability ushered in by the final downfall of Napoleon, made it easier for some writers to make the case for the positive influence that puritanism had exercised in broadening the nation's political and religious freedoms. A key figure in this nineteenth-century reassessment of the conflicts of the seventeenth-century struggles was Thomas Babington Macaulay, whose five-volume *History of England* (1848–61) was one of the most popular works of the century. He justified the actions of the Long Parliament against Charles I and applauded the puritans who had supported the Parliament's defense of English liberties, attributing the success of that cause to their zeal and determination. But like many Victorians, Macaulay was alienated by the religious enthusiasm of the puritans, writing that it masked vindictive feelings. He did much as anyone to establish the popular image of the puritans as sour, gloomy, and intolerant killjoys. It was Macaulay who wrote that puritans objected to bearbaiting not because it inflicted pain on the bear but because it gave pleasure to the spectators.

Much of the discussion about the puritan legacy focused on Oliver Cromwell. Macaulay diverged from the traditional negative judgment of Cromwell, seeing the Lord Protector as someone who strove to balance order and freedom. But the dramatic rehabilitation of Cromwell in the nineteenth century owed the most to Thomas Carlyle's edition of the *Letters and Speeches of Oliver Cromwell* (1845). His own Scottish Calvinist background made Carlyle appreciate the depth of Cromwell's religious commitment and the genuineness of his faith. It was Carlyle who was responsible for the identification of the conflict between Charles I and his Parliament as the *Puritan* Revolution. The authoritarianism of the puritan leader was not criticized but applauded by Carlyle, who was a critic of many of the liberal policies of his own day. Dissenters, who achieved greater political influence in late nineteenth century England, also found much to praise in Cromwell. The fact that he was more tolerant of religious diversity than many of his fellow puritans was a point that in their eyes made him representative of the best in puritanism.

As heirs of the puritan past, Dissenters also emphasized the moral (rather than the theological) elements of the puritan character and pointed to them as worthy of contemporary emulation. If later generations would condemn the puritans for Victorian rigidity, the fault would in part lie with the Dissenters, who had sought to justify their own moral stance by connecting it with the seventeenth-century saints. In a parallel development, Victorian imperialists praised Cromwell's regime for having made England into a formidable military power on the world stage. Many of these themes were brought together in the works of Samuel Rawson Gardiner, who depicted Cromwell as a national hero.

The tercentenary of Cromwell's birth in 1899 saw a variety of celebrations, most organized by Congregationalist and Baptist religious groups. But a plan to place a statue of Cromwell in the Houses of Parliament showed that appreciation of the puritan leader was not universal. Opposition from various sources (particularly the Irish members of Parliament) forced a change in plans. Government funds were not used and the statue was placed outside of Westminster Hall, where it can still be seen today. In the first half of the twentieth century, images of Cromwell and the puritan past continued to be influenced by contemporary politics. In the 1930s some saw in his military dictatorship a foretelling of fascism, while others pointed to the puritans as the early champions of the democratic values that were opposed to fascism. At the same time, Socialist and liberal historians such as Christopher Hill "discovered" the Levellers and found much to praise in their political views.

The twentieth century also saw an attempt to link puritanism to broader movements in the shaping of the modern world. Max Weber's *The Protestant Ethic and the Spirit of Capitalism* (1930 in its English translation) suggested that the psychological effects of predestinarian theology fostered an ethic that fueled economic growth in England and America. While Weber's specific argument has been rejected by most historians, a general link between puritanism and capitalism is still an element in many treatments of the puritans.

The Englishman R. H. Tawney offered his own take on *Religion and the Rise of Capitalism* (1922). But whereas Weber was concerned with how Calvinism influenced the inner life and behavior of individuals, Tawney explored how the capitalist spirit undercut the traditional social ethic, which he believed represented the true spirit of Christianity. In a series of essays, Tawney argued that the Civil Wars were the product of shifts in the distribution of power and property in England.

The American sociologist Robert Merton, in his 1938 essay "Science, Technology and Society in Seventeenth-Century England," argued that puritanism played a key role in the Scientific Revolution. Focusing on those puritans who emphasized the experience of God's grace, he identified this trait as conducive to the experimental orientation of modern science. Critics raised questions about Merton's identification of "puritans," his failure to explain why men who were clearly nonpuritans engaged in scientific research, and why, if the connection was so strong, not all of these puritans were open to scientific investigation.

Christopher Hill influenced a whole generation through his numerous writings on puritanism. A Marxist, Hill shared some of the interests of Weber and Tawney, and argued that there was an affinity between the puritans and the rising middle class. He also followed Merton in connecting puritanism with the rise of science. But Hill was never the captive of any ideology and reveled in exploring unexamined corners of the intellectual and religious landscape, exploring the nuances in the relationship between *Society and Puritanism in Pre-Revolutionary England* (1964), and bringing to the forefront some of the more radical and colorful figures associated with it in *The World Turned Upside Down* (1974).

In the latter half of the twentieth century, new scholarship has transformed our understanding of puritanism as a religious movement. In contrast to earlier works written from narrow, denominational perspectives, scholars such as Geoffrey Nuttall, Patrick Collinson, and Peter Lake have offered us a more nuanced understanding of the nature of puritanism and the Elizabethan puritan movement, which reflects the beliefs and attitudes of the times in which the godly lived. A loosely defined "revisionist" school of historians challenged the long-term significance of the conflict of the 1640s by depicting it as an almost accidental event rather than the consequence of a deep ideological divide. Yet historians such as John Morrill have seen religion as critical in the outbreak of Britain's Wars of Religion. Morrill, along with Conrad Russell, Alan Ford, Jane Ohlmeyer, and others, have also been instrumental in placing these events in a wider British rather than simply English context. Yet despite the sophistication of such studies, academic insights have failed to shift the popular image of puritans as intolerant, bigoted, and censorious.

The puritan legacy in America

In America, the first histories of New England had been written by those who were themselves part of the story. John Winthrop's *Journal* and William Bradford's *Of Plymouth Plantation* were the most significant. Though neither of these was published until the nineteenth century, they were known to those who wrote about early New England. Edward Johnson's *A History of New England* (1653) announced its viewpoint in its subtitle, *The Wonder-Working Providence of Sion's Savior in New England*. William Hubbard and Increase Mather both wrote contemporary accounts of King Philip's War. But it was Cotton Mather's two-volume compilation of history, biography, and piety—the *Magnalia Christi Americana* (1702)—that did the most to pass on to later generations the puritan sense of a special relationship with God and a divinely inspired errand in the wilderness.

The broader puritan religious legacy was revitalized during the Great Awakening of the eighteenth century, which Jonathan Edwards and others saw as a return to the principles of their spiritual ancestors. Elements of that tradition were also evoked in the crisis leading to the American Revolution. The Boston clergyman Jonathan Mayhew drew explicit comparisons between the puritan resistance to the policies of Charles I and the resistance to George III's Stamp Act, on one occasion choosing the anniversary of the execution of Charles I to warn against the tyranny of unlimited power. Samuel Adams wrote a series of articles in the Boston newspapers linking royal policies to popery and chose to sign them "a Puritan." In 1767 John Adams chose to present his objections to Governor Francis Bernard in a series of newspaper essays written in the form of letters from Governor Winthrop to Governor Bradford. And the New Englanders were

A
HISTORY
OF
New-England.

From the Englifh planting in the Yeere
1628. untill the Yeere 1652.

Declaring the form of their Government,
Civill, Military, and Ecclefiaftique. Their Wars with
the Indians, their Troubles with the Gortonifts,
and other Heretiques. Their manner of gathering
of Churches, the commodities of the Country,
and defcription of the principall Towns
and Havens, with the great encou-
ragements to increafe Trade
betwixt them and Old
ENGLAND.

With the names of all their Governours, Magiftrates,
and eminent Minifters.

PSAL. 107.24.
*The righteous fhall fee it and rejoice, and all iniquity fhall ftop her
mouth.*

PSAL. 111.2.
*The works of the Lord are great, and ought to be fought out of all that
have pleafure in them.*

LONDON, *Xen. 29.*
Printed for NATH: BROOKE at the Angel
in *Corn-hill,* 1654. *1653*

10. *A History of New England* was Edward Johnson's providential
interpretation of New England's founding and early history.

well aware of the Atlantic dimension of their puritan past. Samuel Adams was referred to as "the Cromwell of New England," and patriot leaders often gathered at the "Cromwell's Head" tavern in Boston.

Most Revolutionary era evocations of the founders of New England emphasized the puritans' resistance to English oppression rather than their specific religious beliefs. That shift was also evident in two of the early post-Revolutionary historical works that dealt with the puritan legacy. Mercy Otis Warren in her *History of the Rise, Progress and Termination of the American Revolution* (1805) and Abiel Holmes in his *American Annals* (1805) both pointed to New England to praise the virtue of the founders and their contributions to American democracy. This trend was continued in George Bancroft's ten-volume *History of the United States* (1834–75) and John Gorham Palfrey's five-volume *History of New England* (1858–90). Even visitors to America acknowledged the significance of the New England past. Alexis De Tocqueville identified the twin puritan commitments to liberty and religion as something that made America unique.

No nineteenth-century writer wrote more about the puritan tradition than Nathaniel Hawthorne, the descendant of one of the judges in the Salem witch trials of 1692. *The Scarlet Letter* (1850) is arguably the book from which most contemporary understandings of seventeenth-century New England have been drawn. The story of Hester Prynne and Arthur Dimmesdale raises issues of individual freedom and honesty, as well as the community's right to impose communal standards. Hawthorne was deeply immersed in the writings of the puritans, and in works such as *The Scarlet Letter* and "The Minister's Black Veil" he identified what he saw as hypocrisy and narrow-mindedness as key elements of the puritan legacy. But in stories such as "The Grey Champion" Hawthorne wrote in admiration of the puritan tradition of standing up against threats to New England.

At the end of the nineteenth century other descendants of the founders began to take a much sharper tone toward the puritans. Many writers of this Victorian age blamed the puritans for the narrow moralism that they were dissatisfied with. Others, finding that the traditional equation of puritans with liberty did not match what they saw as the reality of seventeenth-century history, focused on the ways in which the puritans had actually denied liberty to others. Reflecting the more secular and Social Darwinist outlook of his own times, Brooks Adams dismissed the religious concerns of his ancestors in *The Emancipation of Massachusetts* (1887). His brother, historian Charles Francis Adams Jr., labeled the puritans a persecuting race in his *Three Episodes of Massachusetts History* (1892).

The tendency to separate as distinct a "religious world" of the puritans and the "political world" of the Revolutionary Era Founders was perhaps most powerfully advanced by Vernon L. Parrington in his *Main Currents in American Thought* (1927), the first two volumes of which won the Pulitzer Prize for historical writing in 1928. For him, clergy such as John Cotton were men frightened by the free spaces of creative thought and "felt safe only behind secure fences, living in a narrow and cold prison of their own devising, and making a virtue of necessity, declaiming on the excellence of those chains wherewith they were bound." Just as at one time the puritans had been applauded for their resistance to the authoritarian English church and state, Parrington and others heralded those who had opposed the puritans as pioneers of religious freedom. There is no statue of John Winthrop or John Cotton on the lawn in front of the Massachusetts State House, but a place was found there for statues of Anne Hutchinson and Mary Dyer despite the fact that they were anything but advocates of the type of pluralism now identified as the key element of American religious freedom.

In the early decades of the twentieth century, puritanism became firmly characterized as a negative influence in American history.

Some writers who had sought to deflect attention from puritan intolerance had focused on their sobriety and unbending morality, but this emphasis was hardly congenial to men and women of the Jazz Age. For the journalist and social critic H. L. Mencken, puritans were not only a people "haunted by the fear that someone, somewhere may be happy," but also people who "not only tried their damnedest to shut out every vestige of sound information, of clean reasoning, of ordinary self-respect and integrity; they absolutely *succeeded* in shutting these things out." Mencken also played a role in the conflation of puritanism with early twentieth-century fundamentalism. This too became a feature of the popular image of the puritans, whereby they were identified with the Scopes trial and Prohibition among other things. During World War I, the anarchist and social critic Emma Goldman lashed out at "The Hypocrisy of Puritanism," claiming that puritanism was based on a Calvinist view that life was a curse from God, referring to puritan rule in England as a "reign of terror," accusing puritans of perverting "the significance and functions of the human body," and charging puritanism with still having "a most pernicious hold on the minds and feelings of the American people."

A scholarly reassessment of the puritans began in the 1930s with the work of the historian Samuel Eliot Morison and continued with the efforts of Perry Miller, Edmund S. Morgan, and others. Reminded of the darker side of human nature by the events of the Holocaust and the Neo-Orthodox theological writings of Reinhold Niebuhr and others, some Americans became more open to assessing the puritans on their own terms. But, as Morison reflected, most Americans still regarded "the fathers of New England as a set of somber killjoys whose greatest pleasure was preventing simple folk from enjoying themselves, and whose principal object in life was to repress beauty and inhibit human nature." It is no surprise that when the playwright Arthur Miller wanted to portray a repressive and persecuting society as a way of commenting on the McCarthyism of the 1950s, he chose to place his play, *The Crucible*, in 1692 Salem.

The modern heritage industry has done little to change these perceptions. Celebrations of the 300th and 350th anniversaries of Massachusetts centered on the overall history of the commonwealth rather than on its founding and early years. The 350th was focused far more on the Boston of Paul Revere than that of John Winthrop. The re-creation of Salem's first settlement (named the "Pioneer Village" rather than the less appealing "Puritan Village") was America's first living history museum. It was briefly popular after its opening in conjunction with the 1930 celebrations of the tercentenary of Massachusetts, but attracted few visitors over the subsequent decades. Salem finds it more profitable to sell its witchcraft heritage than that of the early puritan settlement. Plimoth Plantation is a wonderful living history museum that depicts the lives of the Pilgrims effectively, but there is little focus on their religion as opposed to other aspects of culture and a growing interpretive focus on the Wampanoag natives of the region.

The late twentieth-century re-emergence of religion as an important force in American domestic politics and on the international scene has led to a new interest in the puritan past. Yet despite the fact that numerous political figures, including Presidents John F. Kennedy and Ronald Reagan, have often quoted John Winthrop's "Christian Charity"—the "City on a Hill" sermon—outdated and erroneous stereotypes continue to dominate the popular understanding of puritanism. The prominence of the Religious Right in late twentieth century American politics has led to efforts to denigrate that movement by linking it to revived negative stereotypes of puritanism. The Federal Communications Commission has been attacked for "puritanism" as a result of its efforts to curb what many perceive as indecency on TV and in radio broadcasting. Attorney General John Ashcroft was mocked as a "puritan" for ordering nude statues in the Justice Department covered up, for holding daily prayer meetings, and for authorizing prying into the private lives of Americans. The effort to reshape the American courts has been depicted as a campaign to bring us back to the Mosaic code as espoused by the puritans.

The story of the puritans and their legacy remains a reference point as Americans debate the meaning their past has for their future, as signaled by recent books such as George McKenna's *The Puritan Origins of American Patriotism* (2007) and Andrew R. Murphy's *Prodigal Nation: Moral Decline and Divine Punishment from New England to 9/11* (2008). To a lesser extent the same is true in England. For such discussions to be meaningful it is important to distinguish the actual world of John Winthrop, Anne Bradstreet, and Oliver Cromwell from the misperceptions that have been and may still be shaped for polemical purposes.

References

Introduction

H. L. Mencken, *A Mencken Chrestomathy* (New York: Knopf, 1949), 624.

Chapter 1

Patrick Collinson, *From Cranmer to Sancroft* (London: Hambeldon, 2006), 26.

Chapter 2

The New England Primer (Boston, 1688).

Chapter 4

Richard Baxter, *Reliquiae Baxterianae, or, Mr. Richard Baxter's Narrative of the Most Memorable Passages of His Life* (London, 1696).

Chapter 5

Anne Bradstreet, "Meditations Divine and Moral," in *The Works of Anne Bradstreet*, ed. Jeannine Hensley (Cambridge, MA: Harvard University Press, 1967), 286.

Chapter 7

Vernon Lewis Parrington, *Main Currents in American Thought: An Interpretation of American Literature from the Beginnings to 1920* (New York: Harcourt, 1946), 12.

Emma Goldman, *Anarchism and Other Essays* (Mother Earth Publishing: 1917), 173–74.

H. L. Mencken, *A Mencken Chrestomathy* (New York: Knopf, 1949), 624.

H. L. Mencken, *The Smart Set* (New York: Ess Ess Publishing Co., 1919), 53

Samuel Eliot Morison, *Those Misunderstood Puritans* (North Brookfield, MA: Sun Hill Press, 1992), 3.

Further reading

General works

Bremer, Francis J., and Tom Webster, eds. *Puritans and Puritanism in Europe and America: A Comprehensive Encyclopedia*. 2 vols. Santa Barbara, CA: ABC-Clio, 2006.

Coffey, John, and Paul Lim, eds. *The Cambridge Companion to Puritanism*. Cambridge: Cambridge University Press, 2008.

Foster, Stephen. *The Long Argument: English Puritanism and the Shaping of New England Culture*. Chapel Hill: University of North Carolina Press, 1991.

Chapter 1

Collinson, Patrick. *The Elizabethan Puritan Movement*. London: Jonathan Cape, 1971.

—— . *The Birthpangs of Protestant England: Religious and Cultural Change in the Sixteenth and Seventeenth Centuries*. New York: St. Martin's Press, 1988.

Collinson, Patrick, John Craig, and Brett Usher, eds. *Conferences and Combination Lectures in the Elizabethan Church: Dedham and Bury St. Edmunds, 1582–1590*. Woodbridge, UK: Boydell, 2003.

Kaufman, Peter. *Thinking of the Laity in Late Tudor England*. South Bend, IN: University of Notre Dame Press, 2004.

Lake, Peter. *Moderate Puritans and the Elizabethan Church*. Cambridge: Cambridge University Press, 1982.

Chapter 2

Como, David. *Blown by the Spirit: Puritanism and the Emergence of an Antinomian Underground in Pre-Civil War England.* Stanford, CA: Stanford University Press, 2004.

Durston, Christopher, and Judith Maltby, eds. *Religion in Revolutionary England.* Manchester, UK: Manchester University Press, 2006.

Hughes, Ann. *Gangraena and the Struggle for the English Revolution.* Oxford: Oxford University Press, 2004.

Lake, Peter. *The Boxmaker's Revenge: "Orthodoxy," "Heterodoxy," and the Politics of the Parish in Early Stuart England.* Manchester, UK: Manchester University Press, 2001.

Moore, Susan Hardman. *Pilgrims: New World Settlers and the Call of Home.* New Haven, CT: Yale University Press, 2007.

Morrill, John. *Oliver Cromwell.* Oxford: Oxford University Press, 2007.

———. *The Nature of the English Revolution: Essays.* London: Longmans, 1993.

Norton, Mary Beth. *In the Devil's Snare: The Salem Witchcraft Crisis.* New York: Knopf, 2002.

Spurr, John. *English Puritanism, 1603–1689.* Basingstoke, UK: Macmillan, 1998.

Tyacke, Nicholas. *Anti-Calvinists: The Rise of English Arminianism.* Oxford: Oxford University Press, 1987.

Webster, Tom. *Godly Clergy in Early Stuart England: The Caroline Puritan Movement, c. 1620–1643.* Cambridge: Cambridge University Press, 1997.

Winship, Michael. *Making Heretics: Militant Protestantism and Free Grace in Massachusetts, 1636–1641.* Princeton, NJ: Princeton University Press, 2002.

Chapter 3

Bozeman, Theodore Dwight. *The Precisionist Strain: Disciplinary Religion and Antinomian Backlash in Puritanism to 1638.* Chapel Hill: University of North Carolina Press, 2004.

Cohen, Charles. *God's Caress: The Psychology of Puritan Religious Experience.* New York: Oxford University Press, 1986.

Godbeer, Richard. *Sexual Revolution in Early America.* Baltimore: Johns Hopkins University Press, 2002.

McGiffert, Michael. "Grace and Works: The Rise and Division of Covenant Divinity in Elizabethan Puritanism. *Harvard Theological Review* 75 (1982), 463–502.

Moore, Jonathan. *English Hypothetical Universalism: John Preston and the Softening of Reformed Theology.* Grand Rapids, MI: Eerdmans, 2007.

Wallace, Dewey. *Puritans and Predestination: Grace in English Protestant Theology, 1525–1695.* Chapel Hill: University of North Carolina Press, 1982.

Chapter 4

Daniels, Bruce. *Puritans at Play: Leisure and Recreation in Colonial New England.* New York: St. Martin's, 1996.

Eales, Jacqueline, and Christopher Durston, eds. *The Culture of English Puritanism, 1560–1700.* New York: St. Martin's, 1996.

Gildrie, Richard. *The Profane, the Civil, and the Godly: The Reformation of Manners in Orthodox New England, 1679–1749.* University Park: Penn State University Press, 1994.

Hall, David. *Worlds of Wonder, Days of Judgment: Popular Religious Belief in Early New England.* New York: Knopf, 1989.

Hambrick-Stowe, Charles. *The Practice of Piety: Puritan Devotional Disciplines in Seventeenth-Century New England.* Chapel Hill: University of North Carolina Press, 1982.

Seaver, Paul. *Wallington's World: A Puritan Artisan in Seventeenth-Century London.* Stanford, CA: Stanford University Press, 1985.

Chapter 5

Foster, Stephen. *Their Solitary Way: The Puritan Social Ethic in the First Century of Settlement in New England.* New Haven, CT: Yale University Press, 1971.

Cooper, James F., Jr. *Tenacious of Their Liberties: The Congregationalists in Colonial New England.* New York: Oxford University Press, 1995.

Crawford, Patricia. *Women and Religion in England, 1500–1720.* London: Routledge, 1993.

Johnson, James. *A Society Ordained by God: English Puritan Marriage Doctrine in the First Half of the Seventeenth Century.* Nashville, TN: Abingdon, 1970.

Macfarlane, Alan. *The Family Life of Ralph Josselin, a Seventeenth-Century Clergyman: An Essay in Historical Anthropology.* Cambridge: Cambridge University Press, 1970.

Morgan, Edmund S. *The Puritan Family: Religion and Domestic Relations in Seventeenth-Century New England.* Rev. ed. New York: Harper, 1956.

Porterfield, Amanda. *Female Piety in Puritan New England.* New York: Oxford University Press, 1992.

Reis, Elizabeth. *Damned Women: Sinners and Witches in Puritan New England.* Ithaca, NY: Cornell University Press, 1997.

Wrightson, Keith, and David Levine. *Poverty and Piety in an English Village: Terling, 1525–1700.* Rev. ed. Oxford: Clarendon, 1995.

Chapter 6

Breen, Timothy. *The Character of the Good Ruler: A Study of Puritan Political Ideas in New England.* New Haven, CT: Yale University Press, 1974.

Coffey, John. *Persecution and Toleration in Protestant England, 1558–1689.* Harlow, UK: Longman, 2000.

Cogley, Richard. *John Eliot's Mission to the Indians before King Philips War.* Cambridge, MA: Harvard University Press, 1999.

Haigh, Christopher. *The Plain Man's Pathways to Heaven: Kinds of Christianity in Post-Reformation England.* Oxford: Oxford University Press, 2007.

Hall, Timothy L. *Separating Church and State: Roger Williams and Religious Liberty.* Urbana: University of Illinois Press, 1998.

Hill, Christopher. *The World Turned Upside Down: Radical Ideas during the English Revolution.* London: Temple Smith, 1972.

Murphy, Andrew. *Conscience and Community: Revisiting Toleration and Religious Dissent in Early Modern England and America.* University Park, PA: Penn State University Press, 2001.

Vaughan, Alden T. *New England Frontier: Puritans and Indians, 1620–1675.* 3rd ed. Norman: University of Oklahoma Press, 1995.

Walsham, Alexandra. *Charitable Hatred: Tolerance and Intolerance in England, 1500–1700.* Manchester, UK: Manchester University Press, 2006.

Chapter 7

Arch, Stephen. *Authorizing the Past: The Rhetoric of History in Seventeenth-Century New England.* De Kalb: Northern Illinois University Press, 1994.

Greaves, Richard. *John Bunyan and English Nonconformity.* London: Hambeldon, 1992.

Keeble, Neil. *The Literary Culture of Nonconformity in Later Seventeenth-Century England.* Leicester, UK: Leicester University Press, 1987.

McKenna, George. *The Puritan Origins of American Patriotism.* New Haven, CT: Yale University Press, 2007.

Worden, Blair. *Roundhead Reputations: The English Civil Wars and the Passions of Posterity.* London: Allen Lane, 2001.

Index

Index

Visit the
VERY SHORT
INTRODUCTIONS
Web Sites

www.oup.com/uk/vsi
www.oup.com/us

➤ **Information** about all published titles

➤ News of **forthcoming books**

➤ **Extracts** from the books, including titles
   not yet published

➤ **Reviews** and views

➤ **Links** to other **web sites** and main OUP
   web page

➤ Information about **VSIs in translation**

➤ **Contact** the editors

➤ **Order** other **VSIs** on-line

MORMONISM
A Very Short Introduction
Richard Lyman Bushman

Beginning with a handful of members in 1830, the church that Joseph Smith founded has grown into a world-wide organization with over 12 million adherents. *Mormonism: A Very Short Introduction* explains who the Mormons are: what they believe and how they live. Written by Richard Lyman Bushman, an eminent historian and practicing Mormon, this compact, informative volume ranges from the history of the Church of Jesus Christ of Latter-day Saints to the contentious issues of contemporary Mormonism. Bushman argues that Joseph Smith still serves as the Mormons' Moses and how their everyday religious lives remain rooted in the conceptions of true Christianity. The book also examines polygamy, the various Mormon scriptures, and the renegade fundamentalists who tarnish the LDS image when in fact they are not members.

"Professor Bushman [is] the nation's chief defender and explainer of Mormonism."

Ramin Rahimian, *The New York Times*

"An elegant, even-handed introduction."

Catholic Herald

"Bushman is clearly the master of this subject and, predictably, he nails the topics accurately and judiciously without special pleading or defensiveness. His treatment of important topics is highly original and at times provocative."

Terryl Givens, author of *People of Paradox: A History of the Mormon Culture*

www.oup.com/uk/isbn/978-0-19-531030-6